TRANSFORMATIONAL
MANAGEMENT

SERIES ON ECONOMETRICS AND MANAGEMENT SCIENCES

This is one of a series of books on econometrics and the management sciences sponsored by the IC^2 Institute of the University of Texas at Austin, under the general editorship of W. W. Cooper and Henri Theil. In this series, econometrics and management sciences are to be interpreted broadly, providing an opportunity to introduce new topics that can influence future activities in these fields as well as allow for new contributions to established lines of research in both disciplines. The books will be priced to make them available to a wide and diverse audience.

Volumes in the Series:

Volume 1: EXPLOITING CONTINUITY: Maximum Entropy Estimation of Continuous Distributions, by Henri Theil and Denzil G. Fiebig

Volume 2: CREATIVE AND INNOVATIVE MANAGEMENT: Essays in Honor of George Kozmetsky, edited by A. Charnes and W. W. Cooper

Volume 3: TRANSFORMATIONAL MANAGEMENT, by George Kozmetsky

TRANSFORMATIONAL MANAGEMENT

Volume 3 of Series on
Econometrics and Management Sciences

GEORGE KOZMETSKY

1985

BALLINGER PUBLISHING COMPANY
Cambridge, Massachusetts
A Subsidiary of Harper & Row, Publishers, Inc.

Chapter 8, "Perspectives on the Human Potential in Technological Change" was excerpted from *Work, Organization and Technological Change*, edited by Gerhard O. Mensch and Richard J. Niehaus (New York: Plenum, 1982). Reprinted with permission.

International Standard Book Number: 0-88730-016-2

Library of Congress Catalog Card Number: 84-24219

Printed in the United States of America

Library of Congress Cataloging in Publication Data

Kozmetsky, George.
    Transformational management.

    (Series on econometrics and management sciences; v. 3)
    Includes index.
    1. Management. 2. Decision-making. I. Title. II. Series.
HD31.K655 1985   658.4   84-24219
ISBN 0-88730-016-2

To Greg and Cindy, Nadya and Mike, Aaron, Bethany,
Daniel, Jordan, Sarah, Taylor, and Caitlin

CONTENTS

PART III   TRANSFORMING THE FUTURE

LIST OF FIGURES

LIST OF TABLES

PREFACE

Today's environment for managing change is fundamentally different from even a decade ago in two key respects. First, the process of change itself has been dramatically accelerated. Science and technology are altering the very nature of American society. Second, a "new economy" is emerging as a result of intense global competition. The old economy emphasized cheap and abundant natural resources, borrowing over savings, growth over efficiency, and quantity over quality. The new economy is reversing these trends. International competition is taking the form of a worldwide scientific, technological, and economic race for preeminence.

Traditional management decisionmaking centered on efficiency and effectiveness. Transformational management must focus more directly on flexibility and adaptability to deal with change. Consequently, there is a pressing need to recognize and apply newer managerial styles, approaches, and methods.

America's business strength has always been its ability to be scientifically creative, technologically adept, entrepreneurially daring, and managerially innovative. To date, the scientific, economic, political, and cultural changes in the enterprise system have not been viewed holistically. Consequently, business managers have had a difficult time evaluating and assessing their impacts on American society. They have had a difficult time monitoring structural growth and functional improvements. They have had a difficult time bringing together knowledge for risk-assessment, productivity, optimum in-dustry structure, technological alternatives, and scientific and tech-nological catch-up and leap-frog. Only by developing an integrative and cohesive framework is it possible to direct business organizations toward information requisitions, innovations, and decisionmaking in a dynamic environment.

Technology and ideology are societal drivers, catalysts that change the composition of society—including its institutions and mecha-nisms of allocation, choice, and transformation. They have dramatic impacts on the nation, individual states, local communities, and busi-ness firms. They affect the viability of our industries, the growth and survivability of our business enterprises, and the role, scope, and pur-pose of emerging private and public sector institutions.

Solutions to critical business issues and problems now demand an integrated, holistic, flexible management that blends technological, managerial, scientific, socioeconomic, cultural, and political consid-erations in an atmosphere of extreme time compression. This is the role of and scope for transformational management.

ACKNOWLEDGEMENTS

A great many people have aided in and contributed to my understanding of transformational management—in fact, far too many to
list here. Nevertheless, there are some friends and colleagues whose
input has been especially insightful and helpful.

I would like to express my appreciation to my colleagues at The
University of Texas at Austin, Eugene Konecci, William W. Cooper,
Abraham Charnes, Isabella C. M. Cunningham, Timothy W. Ruefli,
Elspeth and Walt Rostow, Reuben R. McDaniel, Jr., Robert A. Peter-
son, Kenneth Land, Vic Arnold, Jim Brown, and Seymour Schwartz,
and to my graduate students, particularly Nguyen thi Phoung-Dung,
Michael Gill, Camille Clark, Robert Oliver, and Andrew Wiener.

My appreciation also goes to Senators John Tower and Lloyd
Bentsen of Texas and Congressman Don Fuqua of Florida, Jess
Poore, J. R. Kirkland, George Patten, and Robert Kuhn.

I have gained valuable critical discernment from my association
with Charles Hurwitz, Gregory Kozmetsky, Henry Singleton, Fran
Dedona, William Leone, Barry Munitz, Aurelio Madraza, Richard
Maullin, E. F. Heizer, Jr., Gene Amdahl, Eugene White, John Lewis,
Takuma Yamamoto, Naoya Ukai, Sam Barshop, Jack Wrather,
Edward Gistaro, H. E. O'Kelly, and Admiral B. R. Inman.

From the IC^2 Institute, I would like to acknowledge Harvey Mc-
Mains, Ophelia Mallari, Patricia L. Roe, and Myrna Braziel.

I would like to note my special personal appreciation to Raymond W. Smilor, Associate Director of the IC^2 Institute.

I am grateful to Carol Franco, senior editor at Ballinger Publishing Company, and her staff for their support and assistance.

Ronya Kozmetsky deserves a very special acknowledgment. Her counsel, astute observations, and innovative contributions during the course of developing this book have been immeasurable. Without her, this book would not have been possible.

INTRODUCTION
The Need for Transformational Management

Change is sweeping through American society. Who will lead this change? Who will direct the transformation that is taking place in our society? The attitudes and concerns of the next generation of Americans toward family, jobs, national security, the workplace, the role of governments, business, labor, unions, churches, schools, community organizations, and professional and scientific societies will affect the course of business enterprises. Their beliefs and desires in the next decade will force institutions to transform themselves. In this sense today's managers will need to develop their abilities and skills to become our nation's transformational managers. It is they who will need to innovate, to modify today's institutions and to create new institutions that will reshape societal value systems and goals for a better society.

Transformational management is the process of moving from one state and level of activity and commitment to another. It requires a focus on higher aspirations and longer range views that not only benefit individual firms and corporations but at the same time help provide for the general welfare. Transformational management is focused on social consciousness as well as on decisionmaking. It deals with monitoring, delineating, and clarifying the possibilities for business success in conjunction with the hopes for a better future for society. It consists of getting people and organizations to undertake willingly the challenges of transforming dreams into realities.

1

It is important to distinguish between traditional business management and transformational management. The traditional view of managerial functions consists of future direction (*strategy*), organization (*structure*), and the orchestration of the functions that result in excellent performance (*system*). In addition to these functions, transformational management consists of the manner by which top management communicates with the organization and establishes cultural synergy (*style*). Style is the process by which unique organizational cultures and societal values come together to form mutually agreeable ways of determining social responsibility and accountability both internally and externally to the firm. Another attribute of transformational management is the "people side," the socialization and development process of molding employees and managers into effective and acceptable performers (*staff*). Each organization has its own unique competencies and dominating attributes; these are called *skills*. A final attribute for transformational management involves the aims and aspirations for which the institution stands (*shared goals*).

Key issues resulting from the factors in transformational management area are as follows:

1. Can traditional managers become transformational managers?
2. Can society develop more transformational managers?
3. Are American society and culture ready for transformational managers?
4. Are we able to develop the attributes of transformational management in time to meet changing societal demands?
5. Can we educate transformational managers?

This book is designed to assist business managers to sort out their own values, assumptions, desires, and individual and corporate commitments and dedication to becoming tomorrow's transformational managers. It consists of three parts: Part I—Business and Society, Part II—Technology as a Transformational Resource, and Part III—Transforming the Future.

Part I focuses on factors upon which to build a foundation for transformational management. It deals specifically with society's responsibility to business, business accountability, and corporate governance, and the nature of American ideology.

Society is a composite of many interrelated institutions. As a response to change, society determines which institutions it needs as well as the breadth and scope of its institutions, particularly its business entities.

Legitimizing the power of a corporation depends on its ability to legitimize the structure of its governance. The structure must embrace the future. Accountability must go further than the traditional scope of financial audits. It must embrace the concepts of compliance and comprehensive audits. Comprehensive audits examine all phases of management's responsibilities and activities that deal with long-range plans, manner of governance, the firm's contributions to society's general welfare and managerial effectiveness, efficiency, adaptability, and flexibility.

Accountability for corporate power is the key issue. Most Americans believe that *anyone* who exercises power needs to be accountable. This underlying fear of power suggests those holding unaccountable power can over time become autocratic, arbitrary and arrogant. Power then becomes self-serving rather than serving the larger business and public good.

Ideology is a critical component of culture. As a societal driver it has two key facets. First, it is a systematic body of concepts specifically addressing life or culture. Second, it is a set of integrated assertions, theories, and aims that constitute a generally acceptable sociopolitical and economic body of thought.

The origin and sources of the components of American capitalism as an ideology are difficult to trace historically. Because of the diversity of meanings associated with the term, it would be difficult to tie all the underlying concepts into a single, coherent definition. Yet most American scholars would probably concur that the components of capitalism are economic, political, social, and technological.

The *economic* component includes elements such as private property and ownership, competition, and free enterprise. The *political* component includes elements such as freedom, lack of coercion, voluntarism, and checks and balances. The *social* component includes the elements dynamism, natural laws, ethics, and values. The *technological* component includes the elements innovation, invention, efficiency, quality in production, and cost reduction.

Transformational management seeks to understand the larger ideological nature of American society. The relationship of business to society is inextricably woven into the fabric of external relationships and internal operations. Only by integrating ideology, external relationships, and internal operations can business firms respond positively to the overall changes that are transforming American society.

Part II deals with the commercialization of technology resources. Commercialization is the process by which advances in research and development are transferred to the marketplace, where their impact is felt by society. The commercialization of technology is of paramount importance in restructuring the American economy. For some time the majority of basic research in the United States has been funded by U.S. Department of Defense (DOD). In the past such public funding was viewed as an expenditure rather than an investment in the future. Private sector funding for research and development has been burdened with the same attitudes. The commercialization of research and development (R&D) can play a pivotal role in the transition to the Fourth Industrial Revolution.

Transforming the Fourth Industrial Revolution cluster of innovations into the marketplace is a complex phenomenon. It is not simply adapting a technology to the production of a product or service. The technologies are so numerous and interrelated that integration is the key element for success. The better that management can integrate these in a commercialization process, the more effective will be the chain reaction for business development and the stronger the competitive market position. As a result, a critical dimension for transformational management in commercialization is not simply keeping up with the myriad advances and potential breakthroughs in science and technology. The critical dimension is far more than what used to be referred to as the "information explosion"; it is a "science and technology integration explosion."

A major contributor to a stronger and a more balanced economy is the development of national and state policies as well as private sector strategies that nurture technologies, that encourage emerging industries, and that renew the basic industries in an internationally competitive market. The proper joint cooperative efforts among the federal government, state, and local governments, universities and colleges, other nonprofit institutions, and the private sector can be the multiplying factor for more balanced, stable growth in America.

Three examples of how technology can be used as a transformation resource at the firm level are presented in Part II. One example focuses on the impact of technology on changes in managerial decisionmaking, managerial control, risk analysis, comprehensive audits, and managerial educational improvement possibilities. A second example concentrates on the use of hardware and software technology to transform steel and other basic industries for global competition. The third example addresses the problem of maintaining of U.S. preeminence in the emerging supercomputer industry with a focus on the difference between scientific and economic preeminence.

What emerges clearly from the analysis on these examples is the importance for transformational managers to understand the commercialization process and to utilize technology resources more effectively. When technology is viewed as a resource within a transformation process, management can become more internationally competitive and can delineate more clearly the constraints in the global marketplace. Policymakers in the private and public sectors can then more clearly define critical business and societal issues, generate alternative and coherent solutions, and create feasible initiatives that actually solve problems. Furthermore, the utilization of technology as a resource solves today's managerial paradox. The paradox is that innovation interferes with existing operations, yet if not adapted, it leaves the firm with obsolete products and processes.

Part III establishes that two critical elements are required to transform the future. First, we must truly utilize our great human potential in technological change. Second, we must develop creative and innovative management to meet the demands of a tremendously dynamic world society.

Transformational management is grounded in the belief that leadership makes a significant difference in the way business responds to and copes with change. It is deeply involved with creating real economic value and with adapting the personal aspirations of others to the evolving objectives of the firm and to the larger goals of American society.

Dramatic changes in work activities and organizational structures are already underway. Technology is the driver behind these developments. Over the next decade, technology will be increasingly viewed as a national and world resource, as a generator of wealth, as a means to increase productivity and international trade, as an area for assessment of private and public risk-taking, and as a key factor for improving the organization, education, and training of the work force.

In this context transformational management must be both creative and innovative. The creative functions relate to new conceptions, ideas, methods, styles, and organizational structures, which renew existing organizations and identify emerging industries. Creative management initiates newer modes of managerial planning and control, manufacturing, financing, and marketing, as well as future prospects of scientific advances and possible adaptation of technology.

Innovative functions of transformational management involve abilities to implement, to make things happen, to act immediately and in the long term. Innovative management does more than streamline the operations of a firm to predictable shorter term results. It makes "practical" the creative visions, ideas, and ideals that permit all persons to go beyond their capabilities to achieve a better tomorrow in an organized way. It is the joining of these creative and innovative functions that brings about the newer dimensions of transformational management.

BUSINESS AND SOCIETY

1 SOCIETY'S RESPONSIBILITY TO BUSINESS

The rules and guidelines by which American society exists are in a continuous state of evolution. Today's leadership of all our institutions faces fearful and awesome times. Leaders of the Renaissance, the Reformation and the Industrial Revolution did not have to cope with changes of the same kind and magnitude. Change in those periods was comparatively leisurely and deliberate. The base of power and responsibilities was transformed at a pace that allowed most leaders to comprehend and prepare for change.

Today's leadership has little time to comprehend or prepare for change. These leaders operate in an environment of unrelieved crises, confrontations, disorder, exploitation, and pending disaster. Too often today's leaders don't know which way to lead or how to move the requisite institutions, organizations, and the public. They have a difficult time understanding the complex interaction of our individual value systems with the generally accepted rules and guidelines under which each major institution in American society operates.

The establishment of separate policies by each institution becomes part of the nation's cultural, political, and economic process. Achievements arising from these policies have led to economic affluence, advanced science, and technology and have provided a multiplicity of economic, social, and cultural benefits for each American. The consequences of achieving our broad goals are stated succinctly by Max Ways:

> Looking back, we can all think of massive horrors that would have been averted or, at least, ameliorated if the Industrial Revolution had been guided more intelligently by the societies that gave it birth and nurture. None of these societies probed vigorously enough or soon enough to foresee the indirect consequences of the steam engine, the dynamo or the automobile. Because policy making was inadequate, industrial societies slipped into patterns of action that no one had designed or intended—least of all the scientists, engineers and businessmen who were most directly responsible for the innovations that changed society. Neither the Nineteenth Century's squalor nor the Twentieth Century's record of social conflict and environmental pollution had to happen.[1]

Ways questions how society's piecemeal approach of today will lead to stability tomorrow. He suggests that the first step is to determine how society's institutions will contribute to the new rules and guidelines. Individual institutional policymaking precludes the possibility that societal decisionmaking needs to be centralized. Decisionmaking by institutional leaders reflects independent actions for a pluralistic society. Granted they are interdependent. They must therefore discharge their respective institutional responsibilities within some shared framework to lend order and stability.

Society is a composite of many interrelated institutions; it is not composed only of government and business. Neither is social responsibility confined to these same institutions. Society must determine which institutions it needs. Just as hereditary monarchies were exchanged for democratic institutions, so will it be necessary for society to determine the breadth and scope of its institutions. This is not new; American society has added institutions as required, an example being the rise of the unions.

The difference today is that for any change, society must take into account all of its institutions and their simultaneous interrelationships. It cannot continue to hope that societal problems are solved simply by changing the rules under which business, for example, operates as an institution.

Society has a responsibility to business and its other institutions. Abraham Lincoln stated the revolutionary rights of American society as follows:

This country, with its institutions, belongs to the people who inhabit it. Whenever they shall grow weary of the existing government, they can exercise their constitutional right of amending it, or their revolutionary right to dismember or overthrow it.[2]

The stability of society depends on finding solutions for its problems and not on radical changes in values and institutions.

Many clarifications and corrections have been made to delineate business responsibilities to society, and there is still more to be done. But it is also time to reverse the inquiry and ask: What are society's responsibilities to business as an institution?

Before answering, it is necessary to set the stage. Society is not a philosophical construct. It is a reality that consists of human, natural, physical, and technological resources. Society has delegated its institutions to allocate these resources to attain desired conditions. That is why President Lincoln said the *people* are the society and can change the allocation of resources through institutions. The allocation process is not exclusively reserved for judicial, political, or governmental institutions.

Because society gives responsibility for the allocation of resources to its institutions, society must in turn be accountable, making sure to provide the proper policy, guidelines, and authority commensurate with these responsibilities. Ample evidence exists that it is not doing so. The evidence lies in the manner in which various special interest groups have banded together to bring about changes in the rules and guidelines that govern all society's traditional institutions. We are witnessing the multiplication of special interest groups that are concerned with one or more societal problems and try to deviate from society's current guidelines. Because society has not institutionalized many of these special groups, there is no way to make them accountable for their actions. In short, society has not established the criteria necessary to determine if such special groups are acting in the public interest. A simple appeal in the name of public interest is not necessarily adequate for special interest or established institutions. Preserving the public interest means being accountable for the well-being of the majority without violating individual rights under our Constitution. In addition, preserving the public interest must include monitoring the impacts of the special interests upon the currently established institutions. Guarding the public interest demands the distinguishing and choosing between major and minor societal needs. It is the only way society can intelligently guide changes so as to avert massive horrors and their indirect consequences. When society does not take into account the total impact of any change upon business as an institution, it is not discharging its social responsibilities.

Another question—How is U.S. society to provide a framework for order and stability?—brings us back to the earlier questions: Has society delegated too much to its current institutions? Has society assumed a value system for special interests that is not in conformity with its own guidelines? Has society unconsciously abdicated its societal responsibilities to determine policies and guidelines relative to a desired state of society, to active special interests, or to apathetic institutions or to overly dominant institutions?

Too often in the past few years both institutions and special interest groups have assumed unto themselves as decisionmakers all the required policy-setting authority. This has been done without regard to the other institutions and their impacts on the public interest and the constitutional rights of individuals. In many respects, we are living through a period of history both challenging and frightening. The major danger is preoccupation with an uncertain future. There is an equally threatening concept which Coleman McCarthy identified as "present shock":

> The person in shock in the 20th Century is one who is constantly learning of so much tragedy, horror, chaos and absurdity that he can no longer absorb it. He becomes numb. We can stomach so much reality, then we sicken. The great danger of present shock is . . . emotional passivity. It becomes impossible to care about everything, so we wind up caring about nothing.[3]

American society's responsibilities to business as an institution can be clearly set forth within a strategic and dynamic framework. The framework is such that society has the responsibility of safeguarding the public interest and preserving individual freedom. Society then delegates, by the establishment of institutions, how it will effectively utilize our domestic intellectual, natural, and technological resources. It also falls on society to assess whether the institutions have attained the desired state of American society within its proper role in the world. The United States cannot attain its desired state of society under independent self-regulation by each of its institutions or by special interests or even by a few dominating institutions. It is also impossible for the United States to attain its desired state by overtaxing any one institution or individual. Overloading of any regulative institution, whether judicial, executive, or legislative, results in societal confusion and uncertainty, and causes defensiveness and preoccupation with basic individual survival. This then makes it difficult or impossible to create required changes to existing institutions or creating new institutions and rules and guidelines.

In short, such action only serves to perpetuate what Max Ways identified as "policy making [that was] inadequate . . . and slipped into patterns of action that no one designed or intended."

In a 1975 article on journalist Edward R. Murrow, Edward Bliss, Jr. set forth clearly the consequences of such actions.

> He [Murrow] said that if a confused public finally loses faith in America—in those who inform—"Then distrust, dissatisfaction, fear and laziness can combine to turn them in desperation to that 'strong man' who can take them only to destruction."
>
> In his McCarthy broadcast he said, "We will not walk in fear, one of another. We will not be driven by fear into an age of unreason if we dig deep in our history and our doctrine and remember that we are not descended from fearful men."[4]

American society can no longer expect to discharge its own social responsibilities solely by relying on its various regulatory institutions to independently establish rules and guidelines. Governmental institutions alone cannot define and prescribe the responsibilities of American business as an institution. The selection of society's form (for example, capitalistic or socialistic) belongs to the people. Government and business institutions are not and cannot be adversaries. For in the words of President Lincoln, the American public has the "right to dismember" or to rearrange both institutions. Within the strategic and dynamic society's framework, they are not competitive. Both are necessary to safeguard the public and individual interest.

In the past American society has provided business certain rules and guidelines. Among these are that business as an institution has a major economic role in our society. Private business as an institution is both the major producer of goods and services and the major employer. Today 81 percent of the people work for private business institutions. Public employment under governmental institutions provide 19 percent of the employment. What is lacking is what business as an institution says is "national policy." Society has a responsibility to business to determine rules and guidelines that delineate the long-term direction of society relative to its human, material, and service needs. These guidelines should deem what business as an institution should provide and be held accountable for, either through self-regulation or governmental or other institutional regulation. In addition, the probable impact of these guidelines should be determined before they are promulgated.

Society has established for business as an institution to provide

1. Required goods and services both on national and international basis
2. Meaningful employment and leisure opportunities within the American society's desired state
3. The delineation of interlinking institutions involving financing, distribution, regulation, and incentives for business as an institution
4. Establishment of an acceptable means and time to delineate the state of business as an institution in an accountable framework to both society and society to business

Business as an institution cannot wait for society to discharge its responsibilities. It cannot be apathetic. It cannot continue to think that simple financial and economic participation in society is enough. Business must assert itself in society and take an active role with other institutions. American business leaders must take the initiative in the establishment of the strategic and dynamic framework for American society. Those leaders must prepare themselves to extend their expertise beyond their business institutions to society's framework as a whole even while extending the basic established principle of free enterprise.

Business leaders must prepare themselves for multi-institutional and societal careers. Financial contributions to other institutions— political, cultural, educational, religious, health and welfare, and charitable—are not enough for today's, let alone tomorrow's, desired stable American society. Rhetoric on economic or political principles has the same limitation. Personal and dedicated interinstitutional participation is necessary.

Business leaders are in a position to set forth the areas that clearly demand the establishment of society's responsibilities to business as well as to all other institutions. Such leaders, along with other institutional leaders, know high-priority issues that require society to take action. Among these issues for American society are the following:

1. Nature of society
   a. Affluent versus effluent
   b. Growth, no growth, or stable growth with conservation, recycling, and development of planetary resources
   c. Profit as a fair return and sufficient to meet the required standards of living for the people while providing sufficient leisure time

2. Human needs
   a. Life-cycle development of individual needs for education, work, leisure, and retirement
   b. Changing the nature of the family by providing work for each member
   c. Improving health care systems and stopping individual or institutional abuses
   d. Protecting and developing civil rights, including individual and community safety from crime

3. Natural resources and environment
   a. Balancing development of natural resources for a healthy economy and improved standard of living
   b. Balancing cost versus benefits of institutional investment for environmental or for a healthy economy, quality of life, and a stable society
   c. Balancing agriculture to meet domestic and international needs in light of available natural resources and desired environment

4. Improving governance
   a. Delineating the role of governments—federal, state, and local—and of the people meeting individual and community needs and goals
   b. Restructuring of the governmental institutions, regulatory and judicial bodies for more effective utilization of human, natural, physical, and technological resources to meet societal needs

    c. Establishing the means for effective accountability of all levels of governmental institutions, including the appropriate required updating of the Constitution

5. Reassessing business and industrial structure
   a. The means of providing required capital resources
   b. Basic communication and transportation of people, goods, and services, including urban and rural requirements
   c. The role of industry or government in urban redevelopment and the development of new required communities
   d. Location of manufacturing industry to attain national, international, and regional economic development
   e. Research, development, and dissemination of technology with requisite incentives
   f. Basic role of U.S. industry in international trade and finance

An examination of academic programs as well as faculty research indicates that too little effort and time are devoted in U.S. graduate schools of business to the role of business institutions in society. Still less effort is applied to delineating the responsibilities of society to business as an institution. In short, we need to utilize our best intellectual powers on capitalism as a constructive force in a free and democratic society if we are to preserve and extend our private enterprise system. Much of the academic focus in graduate schools of business has been on the development of potential business leadership in large organizations. This effort should be continued but augmented by more effort to develop tomorrow's business leadership for a capitalistic society.

American business as an institution in our society needs to reaffirm what our founding fathers embodied in the Tenth Amendment, namely

> The power not delegated to the U.S. by the Constitution, nor prohibited to it to the States, are reserved to the States respectively or *to the people.*

Business needs to emphasize "to the people," because the people make up society.

NOTES TO CHAPTER 1

1. Max Ways, " 'The Question': Can Information Technology Be Managed?" *Information Technology: Some Critical Implications for Decision Making* (New York: The Conference Board, 1972), p. 3.
2. From his First Inaugural Address, March 4, 1861.
3. Coleman McCarthy, " 'Present Shock': We Can Take Only So Much," *Los Angeles Times*, April 2, 1974, Section B, p. 1.
4. Edward Bliss, Jr., "Remembering Edward R. Murrow," *Saturday Review*, May 3, 1975.

2 ACCOUNTABILITY AND CORPORATE GOVERNANCE
A New Perspective

There is a need to lay the groundwork for enhancing the profession of modern accounting, including the independent certified public accountants and the corporate internal auditors. The changes in these professions will be derived from the emerging modern roles and scope of American corporations and their governance. There is no question that corporate governance in the 1980s has taken on newer dimensions of autonomy and accountability. The phrase "accountable enterprise," coined by Peter Drucker, may eventually replace the older phrases of "free enterprise" or "private enterprise."

Legitimizing the power of a corporation will depend on whether we are able to legitimize the structure of its governance. The structure must extend the scope of audits from financial or opinion audits to compliance and comprehensive audits. Compliance audits address themselves to whether the corporation is complying with "generally accepted" financial, legal, and social principles or practices. Comprehensive or full-scope audits of all phases of management's responsibilities and activities will have to deal not only with management effectiveness, manner of governance, and long-range plans, but also the firm's contributions to society's general welfare. The central theme of the newer scope of comprehensive auditing practice was stated by W. W. Cooper and Yuji Ijiri in their book titled, *Eric Louis Kohler: Accounting's Man of Principles:* "The distinguishing characteristic of accountants lies in their expertise in detecting and deter-

19

mining 'accountability relations' and how they should be serviced for a satisfactory functioning of modern society."[1]

Accountability for corporate power is a key issue. Most Americans believe that *anyone* who exercises power needs to be accountable. People fear the indiscriminate exercise of power because they worry that those holding power without accountability may, over time, become autocratic, arbitrary, and arrogant. Power *can* become self-serving rather than serving the public good. One way of attaining accountability is to have those in responsible positions subject to removal for failure to achieve acceptable results. Today, however, it is difficult to find a consensus as to whom major corporation's managers are accountable. Many believe that giant corporations and their managers are not responsible to their owners—the shareholders. On the other hand many shareholders, institutional or individual, are primarily concerned only with their return on investments. And still, there are those convinced that the use of a "free market mechanism" to hold major corporations accountable is not effective. For too long the corporation's survival has been the preoccupation of most corporate management and their boards of directors. They have neglected to assess the firm based on its satisfactory performance in societal terms. Nor have management and boards determined how to quelch the misuse of corporate power. They must decide to move through more voluntary full disclosure or newer governance that reorganizes the office of the chairman and chief executive officer.

CORPORATE GOVERNANCE

The growth of government ownership and regulation of productive wealth must be kept in check by providing a newer form of corporate governance that can be audited in terms of the generally expected accountability. This makes it imperative that the professions in accounting and business reevaluate their tools and functions as well as their role in corporate accountability. Academicians must provide the necessary research and education fot the new requirements of managerial compliance and accountability.

In the mid-1960s the loss of confidence in the leadership of American institutions caused many to question their legitimacy. But loss of confidence is a lot like the weather. Everybody talks about it, is influenced by it, and blames it, but no one can find a way to make anyone accountable. The first institution to feel the impact of the loss of confidence in the 1960s was the family. Children stimulated by virtually constant exposure to information technology, and by their broadening involvement outside the home, began to challenge parental authority and values. They examined their parents' behavior and found that it often compared unfavorably with the rules the parents espoused. They deplored their parents' affluence, dismissing it as ugly materialism, and they challenged the ability of "hypocrites," "materialists," and "corrupt politicians" to be loving and responsible parents.

Here were millions of young people with enormous political, economic, and communications power, questioning not only the tenets of adult society but also the capacity of existing leadership to direct its institutions. *Civil disobedience*, the touchstone of the movement, was channeled into peace marches, civil rights demonstrations, campus rebellions, and, in its more anarchic guises, into various underground guerilla movements.

Establishment leaders were no more prepared to cope with this loss of confidence than were parents. The values of society were changing, and accepted rules no longer applied. The "now generation" was just that—a generation trained to demand immediate gratification and ready answers to unsolved and enduring issues of accountability. This generation had grown up enjoying an excess of excellence, to which the efforts of preceding generations had accustomed them. *Every* American should have a college education and anyone old enough to drive should have a car, they believed. Good health, good environment, adequate housing, plentiful food, abundant resources, and the leisure to enjoy them were the birthright of *every* American. They expected this abundance as a constitutional right for themselves and for those who visibly were denied it. Out of this phenomenon grew an unrealistic—but unchecked—quest for perfection. Faults in business leaders, in educators, in religious leaders, in political figures, and in the "system" itself could not be tolerated. And in a chicken-and-egg relationship, whichever came first, the flaws that could not be tolerated by the perfection-seeking young were often not acknowledged by their less-than-perfect elders. When the flaws inevitably surfaced, they were all the worse for having been "hypocritically" covered up or denied.

U.S. business leaders are just now beginning to evaluate the decade of turmoil that ensued, trying to sort out its influences on society and especially on their corporate governance. In this context the essence of management in the 1980s must be foresight, calculated action, and accountability. The action must be predicated on willingness to become involved with crucial issues. In the balance of this century American managers will contend with the effective implementation of their corporate citizenship through responsible or independently validated governance and comprehensive accountability. Merely providing the media or the public with an independent audit certificate will not suffice.

Harold Williams, past chairman of the Securities and Exchange Commission, in a speech before the Securities Regulation Institute, said,

> Our economic problems are not merely those of poor current performance; but rather of sustained neglect and misjudgment. The United States now has the highest percentage of obsolete plants, the lowest percentage of capital investment and the lowest growth in productivity and savings of any major industrial society. Corporate earnings for which management is responsible are not generating and retaining the resources necessary to maintain their productive capacity and are liquidating, without the awareness of shareholders and often without the awareness even of management or the board.

Corporations are subject to government policies, laws, and regulations that encourage consumption and discourage the savings and investment required to revitalize our productive capacity, develop innovative skills, and incorporate new technologies into the economic mainstream of our nation's general welfare. Measurement systems are inadequate to collect the information needed to establish and determine responsibility or to take appropriate and effective corrective action in both the private and public sectors when it is indicated.

Business executives need to remember that the public's respect and trust cannot be assumed. It must be continually earned by performance that goes beyond those measures recorded in periodic and annual reports and tax statements. The public is showing some doubt as to whether the basic job of providing employment, goods, and services, and continuing to increase productive wealth, which is the real test of the capitalist business system, will continue to work. In several instances business has been rescued by transferring business risk to public risk (Penn–New York Central Railroad, Lockheed, and Chrysler are examples). We must ask ourselves if this is the model for the future. If it is, then we are well on our way to a new business/

public/government relationship much different from the one that has brought us to where we are today.

The change in the climate toward American business is more than simply a result of changing public attitudes and expectations as measured by public polls. It is also a result of the changing character of business itself. These changes must be reviewed and audit procedures determined by independent third parties who have no vested interest in the evaluation. It will be difficult to disentangle changing economic, social, political, technological, environmental, and emotional predispositions from changes in the actual objective assessment using the best available facts. Too often the public's perception lumps all businesses together. What appears to be true for very large corporations is perceived to be true for medium and small corporations. This, of course, does not hold.

The real public concern is that corporate power has the appearance of little or no accountability. It is difficult to link corporate accountability in the marketplace to the firm's performance and value to our general welfare. There are two relevant questions: Who actually governs the corporation? How would we evaluate a corporation's performance?

Many observers would like to say that the corporate boards of directors are changing. That is, boards govern the corporations as well as evaluate their managements' performance. Most large public corporations have changed their form of governance. They have audit committees, with outside directors to assist in their governance and accountability. The audit committees are now considered as the financial "watchdogs" of the business. Depending on the board chairman and his charge, audit committees have a wide variety of duties and responsibilities. However, very few to date have been concerned with compliance and comprehensive audits. Boards of directors, as a rule, do not require their outside auditors or internal auditors to provide them with compliance audits; some financial valuations are not attested by the certified public accountants' review, nor are social audits generally performed. Still fewer require comprehensive audits. Nor are we positive that this is their function.

There should be a twofold approach to these needs. One from the practical point of view should be initiated by the board of directors to take up such specifics as the following: Is the firm complying with all the laws and regulations governing it? How effective have past capital budgets been in meeting the goals of the corporation? How effective is the management compensation package relative to performance against stated short-term and long-term corporate goals and a host of other salient points? These could well become the extended functions of the internal auditor in conjunction with independent legal reviews and financial audits by experts other than accountants.

In addition, the boards of directors must start now to organize themselves to perform functions such as reviewing policies concerning "conflict of interest," political positions or contributions, environmental and social impacts, compliance with existing or pending laws or regulations, capital adequacy and long-range strategy for the firm and monitoring of the chief executive's and management's performance. These types of duties are *not inherent* in the common description of corporate governance by the board of directors. Nor are they in the purview of today's or tomorrow's CPAs. They could well be added duties of the internal auditor who reports as staff to the board of directors.

Effective corporate governance depends on attracting qualified directors who are willing to assume responsibility. Directors of public firms must be willing to accept their positions as a public trust. They must be able to make intelligent and informed decisions, based on experience in both the business world and society. Good directors are a scarce resource. Too bad business schools do not provide formal education on becoming a good director!

Corporate governance, in light of pressures from special interest groups, different government agencies, stockholders, and the marketplace, means an expansion of the traditional board responsibilities to include a new degree of accountability. This will require resources in the form of special staffs, legal and investment advisors, and when needed, special study task forces reporting directly to the board. Corporate internal management and operating personnel will be utilized, but comprehensive audits will dictate a degree of external expert review and analysis.

Corporate management must create an appropriate comprehensive system for evaluation that provides real accountability. The academic community also has a responsibility to do the research required to increase knowledge on compliance and comprehensive audits. It is important for the business schools to lead in this area of national concern. Important issues need to be analyzed, exploratory research undertaken, and commitment made by the academic community for developing appropriate accountability and governance.

NOTE TO CHAPTER 2

1. W. W. Cooper and Yuji Ijiri (eds.), "Accounting and Accountability Relations," *Eric Louis Kohler: Accounting's Man of Principles* (Reston, Va.: Reston Publishing Company, 1979), p. 191.

3 THE STATE OF AMERICAN CAPITALISM
Renewing U.S. Prestige

Less than 200 years ago, capitalism was a revolutionary concept. Capitalism is constructive, and because it is, it breeds a quiet, non-violent revolution. Capitalism has always identified itself with the general welfare of the people; when there was a void brought about by a need or a discontent, the system was capable of filling that void. In America there has been no reason for violent revolution in the French or Russian style, nor for accidental or premeditated revolutions in the manner of Poland and Central America.

American capitalism has always had the strength to change from within in sufficient time to check any need for violent, armed, or premeditated revolution. A 1980 article in *The Economist* titled, "Anti-red Revolutions" stated,

> Karl Marx was right. Working people eventually will revolt against any system of social organization based on exploitation by a single class: feudalism by aristocrats, capitalism by monopolists, now socialism by apparatchiks. The revolt against these bureaucrats is everywhere in train, and this month's new leaders in Poland and China could help decide whether the response will be the one which Marx thought would be usual: first, liberal reforms which are sufficiently inefficient to make things worse; then, violent suppression by the frightened ruling class; then, collapse of those rulers before a 1789 or 1917 revolution. The awkwardness is that, when opposing a 1789 or 1917, nuclear-armed apparatchiks could incinerate half the planet.

> The main concern of bureaucrats everywhere is how to protect their privileges. In Russia and its satellites, these are great: access to hard-currency

27

shops, to opportunities for corruption, to being able to boss people about, to freedom from fear of being hanged by an indignant population from the next lamp post. Anything which threatens these sends a personal tremor right up to the Kremlin, as the Polish strikes have done.

Mr. Gierek's dash for centrally-planned industrialization on borrowed capitalist money had led to shortages and long queues and strikes, Mr. Kania's higher wages and more strictly controlled prices will bring worse shortages and longer queues and fiercer strikes, and then presumably military intervention from a Russian bureaucracy which fears it will one day face similar troubles itself.[1]

It is interesting to note that the nations with the problems enunciated in *The Economist* article are predominantly socialist nations of the Eastern bloc. The United States does not have those problems. Our politicians, businessmen, union leaders, and academicians are not faced with being hanged by an angry populace from the next lamp post. Our citizens do not have to face long queues and strikes. The sickness of the Communist nations of the Eastern bloc has produced a void that constructive capitalism can fill in the battle for people's minds and, thereby, bring about a better world for all people and a renewal of prestige of the United States.

The United States is beginning to prepare itself to take advantage of this worldwide opportunity. We are still necessarily preoccupied with our immediate domestic problems. However, we are beginning to get them behind us and under control.

This nation and other nations of the world are in a period of fundamental social, cultural, and economic change. A need exists to conduct research from the perspective of the private sector and its related academic disciplines to analyze the consequences evolving from this change.

The IC² Institute at the University of Texas at Austin has conducted exploratory research on the state of capitalism in the United States. The research on wealth tried to establish objective criteria to measure the dimensions of wealth in the United States, to measure which sectors own and control the wealth and how effective their management of the wealth is. Although the approach is new to academia, it is a familiar one to business. In business we always check to see if the patient is alive before we treat him or her. If there is no pulse, we devote no additional time or resources to the cadaver. There are no autopsies. In academia, by contrast, there is a good reason to study the anatomy and physiology of cadavers. Academe makes its mistakes and creates opportunities on cadavers.

The research on wealth can be summarized briefly.

1. The economic and social wealth of the United States are currently estimated in eight categories: land, structures, equipment, inventories, research and development, cost of rearing children, training and education, and health care. The objective of the current wealth categories estimation was primarily for productivity analysis. Other wealth categories that have been recognized but never measured include technology, human resources, air and water, and natural resources such as coal reserves, oil, gas, shale, and unused agricultural lands; they were not considered in this study.

2. The IC^2 study departed from the current academic notion of wealth as a measure of the means of production only. Instead, it viewed wealth as the resources allocated to institutions in order to achieve societal goals.

3. The ownership and control of wealth in the United States from 1900 to 1975 had the following pattern.

    a. Of the three institutional sectors—household, business, and government—the ownership of the U.S. wealth changed from 1900 to 1975 as follows:

	1900	1975
Household	51%	59%
Business	46%	30%
Government	3%	11%

The household sector still owns the majority of the wealth in the United States. However, if the 1969–1975 trend of ownership continues, in the year 2000 the government sector could own 40 percent of the total wealth, the household sector could be reduced to 33 percent and the business sector could own only 27 percent. In the year 2005, the government sector could own about 52 percent. But trend extrapolations are not cast in stone; trends are not inevitable unless there is no intervention.

    b. The control of wealth by institutional sectors shifted from 1900 to 1975 as follows:

	1900	1975
Household	39%	42%
Business	56%	43%
Government	5%	15%

The only loser in the control of wealth in the past 75 years was the business sector. The major winner was the government sector.

The extrapolation studies with respect to control of wealth based on the 1969–1975 data show that by the year 2000, the government sector could control 20 percent of the wealth, the business sector could control 50 percent, and the household sector about 30 percent.

In 1975 the United States was a capitalistic society in both owner-ship of wealth and control of wealth. The two private sectors, house-hold and business, owned and controlled 89 percent and 85 percent of the wealth, respectively. If there is no intervention in the 1969–1975 trends of ownership and control, however, the private sector will own 60 percent and control 80 percent of the wealth by the year 2000. Capitalism is still alive and kicking and ready to meet the opportunities presented by the sickness within the more socialistic nations.

The IC^2 Institute's wealth studies showed a need to evaluate the current trends of ownership and control. The transformation of wealth by government, business, and the household sectors could no longer continue under the simple theory that business provided em-ployment, that government provided quality of life and the source of capital, and that the household sector chose by ballot or the invest-ment of its funds which sector it wished to control its wealth.

More important, the study revealed that there has been no signifi-cant academic research on the creation of wealth. Academicians and government statisticians do not measure resources available to create wealth. They do not do so because it is difficult—not because it is unnecessary. Wealth represented by yet to be proven natural re-sources, such as the more effective use of renewable resources and the development of technology and the human ability to utilize these resources effectively is more important that the current preoccupa-tion with the allocation and control of wealth.

All political systems share one common denominator in meeting the societal goals of political freedom, material well-being, and qual-ity of life—and that denominator is *wealth*. Wealth is the key to power in any political system. Its ownership, control, and transfor-mation determine not only the structure of society but also the suc-cess or failure of the system itself.

For the last two decades, American business has placed too much emphasis on the allocation of wealth and the distribution of current income and not enough on creating wealth. Preoccupation with the allocation of wealth inevitably led to adversary relationships between business and government and other special interest groups. These adversarial relationships have created attitudes that must be overcome so that America can renew its national and international prestige.

U.S. wealth is not limited to what many call a zero-sum game—a game that says: I have more wealth, you will have less. That may be true in other nations but not in the United States. Although this nation is not completely self-sufficient in every respect, the wealth represented by the unmeasured resources is overwhelming and gives us the power to solve domestic problems in a way that provides for the continued renewal of American prestige at home and abroad.

We know that our economic and political systems are capable of meeting these challenges, but are the American people as well as its leaders prepared for them?

The stability of the political and economic institutions of a nation is affected by the public's confidence. It is for this reason that public opinion polls are used to take the pulse of the nation and to forecast political votes or attitudes toward various principles and values.

Research conducted by the IC^2 Institute has yielded some clear-cut results that are counterintuitive and counter to the media. Capitalism, when compared to socialism and communism as alternative political systems, was considered decidedly more favorable by the sample of Americans polled by the National Family Opinion Firm (see Table 3-1). Those polled had no question that capitalism was preferable because it is less inflationary, more dynamic, more socially equitable, more efficient in allocation of resources, and more likely to advocate the work ethic than either socialism or communism. Capitalism, according to the poll, also allows more political freedom, produces higher quality products, gives better value for the money, better promotes personnel satisfaction, better promotes technology, promotes higher living standards and gives more freedom of choice. On only one attribute—growth in prominence—did the results show no statistical difference among the three institutions. Respondents felt that there was no difference in the growth in prominence of capitalism, socialism, or communism. This survey confirms that we can well be poised to renew the American system's prestige.

Another IC^2 Institute study surveyed respondents to a Harris poll on their perceptions of capitalism. When this sample was asked to de-

Table 3-1. A Comparison of People's Attitudes Toward Capitalism, Socialism, and Communism.[a]

	Capitalism	Socialism	Communism
Inherently inflationary[b]	4.03	4.26	5.02
Dynamic	2.51	5.13	5.75
Efficient in allocating resources	3.39	4.88	5.46
Allows political freedom	2.71	5.36	6.60
High quality products[b]	3.00	5.12	5.43
Good value for money	3.09	5.22	5.84
Growing in prominence[b]	3.75	3.65	4.03
Promotes personal satisfaction	2.71	5.42	6.22
Socially equitable	3.39	5.16	6.12
Promotes technology[b]	2.06	4.76	4.74
High living standards	2.44	5.44	6.22
Freedom of choice	2.38	5.59	6.60
Advocates work ethic[b]	2.50	4.85	4.78

a. Scale = 1—7: 1 represents greatest agreement with statement; 7 represents greatest disagreement.

b. _____ differences not significant.

Source: IC² Research Data gathered using National Family Opinion Sample.

fine capitalism as a concept compared to free enterprise, private enterprise, and American enterprise, 52 percent of the respondents defined capitalism incorrectly. About 30 percent were unable to define any of the other three capitalistic concepts of free enterprise, private enterprise, and American enterprise (see Table 3-2). *Webster's Dictionary* (1971) defines capitalism as follows:

> Capitalism: An economic system characterized by private or corporation ownership of capital goods, by investments that are determined by *private decision* rather than by state control and by prices, production and the distribution of goods that are determined mainly in a *free market.*

The definition of capitalism encompasses the concepts of free enterprise and private enterprise. (A forthcoming Institute study examines the specific attitudes and perceptions of various survey groups relative to capitalism, free enterprise, private enterprise, and American enterprise.)

It is evident from the research results that public opinion perceives capitalism favorably in spite of some confusion as to what capitalism is and how it relates to other basic concepts such as free and private enterprise. It is time, however, to concentrate our efforts on restor-

Table 3-2. Definitions of Capitalism, Free Enterprise, Private
Enterprise, American Enterprise.

Category	Percentage Responding
Capitalism	
Correct definition	47.5
Incorrect definition	52.5
Free Enterprise	
Correct definition	67.9
Incorrect definition	32.1
Private Enterprise	
Correct definition	72.8
Incorrect definition	27.2
American Enterprise	
Correct definition	68.4
Incorrect definition	31.6

ing the true meaning of capitalism by using our system to do what it
was meant to do: *create wealth* for meeting the needs for freedom,
material well-being, and quality of life for all our citizens. The creation of wealth provides the answers to inflation, unemployment,
security, and productivity.

One way of taking the pulse of a society is to poll its leaders. We
conducted polls of present executives and future leaders and compared their attitudes to the average American. For present executives, we polled over 1,000 Texas business leaders. For future leaders, we polled 2,856 university students attending 28 colleges in 23
different states. We polled their attitudes toward capitalism on five
dimensions (see Table 3-3). The first question was "Does capitalism deny the masses property in life, liberty, and estate?" About
90 percent of the present executives said no; about 64 percent of the
average Americans said no; 53 percent of the future leaders said no.

The second statement in the poll was "A capitalistic system advo-
cates the work ethic and the free market mechanism." Over 96 percent of the present executives agreed; about 67 percent of the average Americans agreed; less than 59 percent of the future leaders
agreed.

The third statement was "A free society can exist under a capitalistic system." About 97 percent of the present executives agreed,

Table 3-3. Attitudes toward Capitalism by Business Students,
Average Americans, and Executives.

		Students	Household	Executives
1. Capitalism denies the	Agree	20.7	15.7	7.0
masses property in life,	Neutral	26.7	19.9	3.5
liberty, and estate.	Disagree	52.6	64.4	89.5
2. A capitalistic system	Agree	58.9	66.5	96.3
advocates the work	Neutral	30.0	22.7	1.5
ethic and the free	Disagree	11.1	10.2	2.2
market mechanism.				
3. A free society can exist	Agree	61.1	64.1	96.8
under a capitalistic	Neutral	23.3	18.0	.9
system.	Disagree	15.6	17.9	2.3
4. Efficient management can	Agree	30.9	33.2	72.3
only be achieved through	Neutral	37.7	41.5	12.3
capitalism.	Disagree	31.4	25.3	15.4
5. Capitalists are entitled	Agree	55.0	59.2	94.7
to the reward of profits	Neutral	28.7	27.4	2.3
because they assume the	Disagree	16.3	13.4	3.0
risk of loss.				

while 64 percent of the average Americans agreed; about 62 percent of the future leaders agreed.

The fourth statement was "Efficient management can only be achieved through capitalism." Only 72 percent of the present executives agreed. In this dimension, only 33 percent of the average Americans agreed, and less than 31 percent of the future leaders agreed.

The fifth statement in the poll was "Capitalists are entitled to the reward of profits because they assume the risk of loss." About 95 percent of the executives polled agreed, while 59 percent of the average Americans and 55 percent of the future leaders agreed. These results definitely disclose a quiet revolution.

You will note that present Texas business executives have a substantially different perception of American capitalism than the average Americans and the future leaders represented by the 2,856 university students polled. I would like to share with you the current business executives' views of capitalism taken from another study performed by the IC^2 Institute.

Capitalism. Executives feel that capitalism is a fundamentally sound economic philosophy but rarely argue its merits. They agree more with its results than the process by which free market pricing and the free market allocation of capital act as mechanisms that maximize productivity. They often deny the cases where the free market is alleged to have failed.

Political philosophy. Civil rights are inseparable from property rights according to executives; the growth of government has been accompanied by an accelerating erosion of property rights.

Society. Executives believe that society is making a host of demands on corporate behavior which cannot be met through the pricing mechanisms. They feel the public school system is not providing the understanding of economics and the free enterprise system essential to an intelligent, concerned, effective and informed citizenry. These executives suspect that universities and their faculty are hostile toward business and are reluctant to support programs other than science and technology. They believe that if the media understood business, a more supportive, rather than critical, attitude would develop.

Government. Executives believe regulation is costly and unproductive and that regulatory agencies have taken on a life of their own. They react to government bureaucrats with unconcealed hostility.

Economy. Consensus about the outlook for the decade is gloomy. Executives agree with the Keynesian forecasters and politicians that our economy is sick. Inflation and energy are the greatest worries, but they are pessimistic about the government's ability to solve such problems.

Macroconcentration. Executives are worried by the current trend in policies that punish firms for success and growth, and by the public's opposition to anything they don't understand, particularly if it is big.

Business Ethics. Cases of executive misconduct are exceptions to the normal and historic behavior, according to the executives who see the media and television as responsible for the current poor public image of the business executive.

Robert Peterson, Professor of Marketing at The University of Texas at Austin, conducted a survey of confidence by average Americans toward capitalism, free enterprise, private enterprise, American

Table 3-4. Survey of Average Americans' Confidence in U.S. Economic and Political Systems.

Amount of Confidence	Capitalism	Free Enterprise	Private Enterprise	American Enterprise	Political System
Great deal	27.5%	24.2%	30.9%	18.9%	7.4%
Quite a lot	33.8%	38.1%	34.5%	35.7%	19.5%
Some	25.3%	29.3%	28.8%	33.9%	37.3%
Very little/ None at all	13.4%	8.4%	5.8%	11.8%	35.8%

Source: IC² national survey of 1,536 middle-class Americans.

enterprise, and our political system. The survey determined the amount of confidence on four bases: a great deal, quite a lot, some, and last, very little or none at all.

The average American has a great deal of confidence in private enterprise (30.9 percent); then capitalism (27.5 percent); then free enterprise (24.2 percent); then American enterprise (18.9 percent); and only 7.4 percent have a great deal of confidence in the political system. Analyses of what the average American has very little or no confidence at all in is, first, our political system (35.8 percent—more than 1 of 3 Americans do not have confidence in our government!); next is capitalism (13.4 percent); next is American enterprise (11.8 percent); then free enterprise (8.4 percent); and last, private enterprise (5.8 percent). There is very little question then that in the battle for the people's minds in America, private enterprise is the winner. The clear loser is the American political system. No wonder then that the average American voter did something about that in November 1980. Since January 20, 1981, it has become increasingly clear that a determined, tough-minded group of politicians, drawn from the ranks of business and the Defense Department, are in place in the U.S. government. They are displaying all the attributes necessary to reshape America's government, economy, and international policies. In many respects they are going about establishing new government policies. These actions can result in moving much of the policy setting from the federal level to the state and local levels. The currently enacted and forthcoming deregulations will also do much to place responsibility for constructive action at the level of industry and individual firms. In other words American business as well as state and local governments will be better situated to meet the needs of their local constituencies. The results can well be the case for a sound reversal of our current economic performance, for increased capital investments in new plants and technology, for increased productivity and quality of goods and services as well as for increased national savings. This could lead to a renewal of the average American's confidence in our political institutions.

The Reagan executive staff has demonstrated two forthright characteristics. The first is their serious determination to undertake the enormous, albeit difficult, tasks associated with altering federal tax structure and federal government's role. The second is their zeal and toughness: zeal to get underway quickly and pragmatically with little patience for failures based on unworkable economic theory or political approaches, and toughness in playing hard ball with foreign policy and international trade with former friends and foes.

The Reagan administration has made it clear that it embraces the goal of making the United States once more a prestigious competitive nation. *Competitive* is the key word. The current battle of the federal budget and regulatory changes are aimed at getting the federal government to establish an environment from which American industry can become more competitive and also one in which the average American can once more regain confidence in the U.S. political system.

Now let us concentrate on the consequences, impacts, and opportunities that can result from the so-called Reaganomics. In this respect, three areas are of particular interest: state and local government, business, and international trade. Their common focus is the president's efforts to remove the federal government as the primary source of sickness of the American economy. In an oversimplified way, we can view Reaganomics as a better balancing of key decision-making between federal and state governments and the private enterprise system. Deregulation or providing block funds from the federal government generally mean that the state governments are given more responsibility and authority.

The procedures by which a successful state government is managed have thus been dramatically changed. If the policymaking were centralized at the federal level, as it long has been, then efficient and effective state government management would be greatly dependent on how it sent about implementing federally imposed policies. When the policy setting and authority are transferred to the state level, a new ballgame begins. Consequently, business leaders need companies' positions on federal and state policies and effectively communicate them to the proper authorities as well as to the people.

To many of us, success in business management has been how to succeed in an environment dominated by federal government regulation and monetary and fiscal policies. I wonder if we are ready for Reaganomics. When it comes to international relations, Reaganomics suggests more than security. It embraces international free trade and the competition for all peoples' minds. It takes security, free trade, and American constructive capitalism to achieve a renewed American prestige, nationally and internationally. International competitiveness is also a cornerstone of Reaganomics. I personally do not want to be colonized under the guise of free trade. Modern colonization implies economic rather than political control over a national government. We all know that American firms are relatively cheap in terms of their stock prices. There is no need to have American firms taken over by foreign firms if American business leaders have confidence in the American government. I don't object to competing with foreign companies, or, for that matter, forming transnational companies to increase the standard of living for all people in the world, or for competing with the Eastern bloc nations. Competition has already given us the requisite personal satisfaction that more than compensates for the emotional and physical and family sacrifices involved in constructive leadership. Money and perquisites alone are not enough to compensate for the sacrifices demanded by the people from its leaders.

It is to be feared that American business leaders will not react quickly enough to fill the voids that Reaganomics can create when it removes the excuses for a sick economy and society because of federal government intervention. If taxes were reduced, savings should be reinvested in productive projects by the private sector and not in unproductive projects or in high-yield and personal assets. In the final analysis how each firm and business leader fills the inevitable voids generated by new federal and state policies will to a large measure determine the renewed prestige of America at home and abroad.

NOTE TO CHAPTER 3

1.   "Anti-red Revolutions," *The Economist*, September 20, 1980.

II TECHNOLOGY AS A TRANSFORMATIONAL RESOURCE

4 THE TRANSFORMATION OF TECHNOLOGICAL RESOURCES TO ECONOMIC WEALTH

Commercialization—the process by which results of research and development are transformed into products for sale in the marketplace—may benefit both through increased scale of production, higher quality, and lower prices. National security concerns must, of course, be taken into consideration to ensure the protection of those technologies exclusively required for defense.

Where applicable, sharing of technology can result in less displacement in labor markets as a result of disarmament, renewed détente, or the loss of markets in declining industries.

A number of emerging technologies can be identified for the 1980s and 1990s. Recently, some academic writers have referred to them as the technologies for the Fourth Industrial Revolution. The first three industrial revolutions can be characterized as follows:

- The First Industrial Revolution was based on technologies for manufacturing textiles, making iron from coke, and supplying power from Watt's steam engine.

- The Second Industrial Revolution was based on the railraods and steelmaking.

- The Third Industrial Revolution was based on electricity, batch chemicals, and the internal combustion engine.

When transformed to commercial products, these technologies provided security, economic prosperity, wealth, and national and international prestige.

Technologies for the Fourth Industrial Revolution include microelectronics, biotechnology, lasers, artificial intelligence and robotics, synthetic materials, waste technologies, and communications. These and other innovations in the next few decades will lead to markets for advanced materials, special application designs, photosynthesis, supercold technology, industrial and scientific instrumentation, robotics, and automated batch and process production. All of these Fourth Industrial Revolution technologies should lead to long-term investments in newer plants and equipment, increased productivity and a stronger U.S. international trade posture. The commercialization of defense research and development can play a pivotal role in the transition to the Fourth Industrial Revolution.

The 1983–1986 outlays for defense R&D test and evaluation are important in this context. They are projected to be $21.4 billion in 1983; $26.3 billion in 1984; $30.0 billion in 1986, $32.6 billion in 1986—a total of over $110 billion. These outlays for the next four years will equal 30 percent of the total federal R&D investments for the past 18 years. These are truly significant investments in future U.S. technological resources. Defense R&D outlays thereby could grow from 49.7 percent of the total federal R&D expenditures in 1982 to 53.7 percent in 1983 to over 64 percent by 1986. These expenditures will result in significant technologies that should be commercialized.

America's future comprehensive security depends on our abilities to support and diffuse through innovation the newer technologies of the 1980s. Through their use, we can strengthen our nation's defense posture while improving our domestic and international economic positions. The emerging technologies can become our nation's newer growth industries that will help to stimulate a robust economy in the balance of the 1980s. Estimates show that in addition to federal investments, those by industry, universities and colleges, and other nonprofit institutions for the 1983–1986 period could result in an investment pool of more than $326 billion, in current dollars. The investment can and should be a major stimulant to our economy. What must still be reviewed is whether the resultant infrastructure will be capable of providing significantly greater employment of the working force, over the whole gamut of skills and education, while at the same time maintaining a balanced economic structure for national defense and prestige.

There are four critical phases to the process of commercialization. First (and perhaps the key factor in the transfer of technological resources), how well can the Department of Defense sponsored technology and other R&D technology be transformed into economic wealth? Second, how well can the DOD and other R&D technologically transformed resources be utilized by basic industries, high-technology industries, federal, state, and local governments, educational institutions, and the service industries to enhance their operations? Only by improving efficiency and effectiveness, demand analysis, rate of return and financial analysis can we measure the success of commercialization. Third, how well have the transformed DOD technological and other R&D investments benefited society over both the short and long terms? This assessment must include the subsequent adaptation of these investments by all our institutions and their impact on national security and economic well-being. Fourth, how can we improve the process of transforming technological resources so that they are more fully utilized by institutions and more readily adapted to meet changing values?

To develop a framework to deal with these phases, this paper presents three distinct but interrelated elements:

1. A selected overview of retrospective and prospective insights on national developments since 1945 and on America's R&D, including defense R&D.
2. An evaluation of the current American economic structure and the R&D investments of basic and high-technology industries.
3. A presentation of concepts and issues for commercialization of technology resources for the 1980s and 1990s.

NATIONAL DEVELOPMENTS SINCE 1945

The period of 1945 to 1982 was one of the great periods of change in American history. It began with a euphoric state of power and unexcelled leadership. Several significant factors characterized the early part of this dramatic era:

1. The United States believed that it could and should police and reorder the world.

2. Americans generally thought that in any context between good and evil, good would prevail. Moreover, the United States could decide what was good or bad.

   a. Politically, we had a moral mandate not to let evil happen again in the world.
   b. Economically, we would spend whatever it took to preserve good regardless of what it cost the American people.

3. Scholars played an important part in the war and could never again be ignored in American life.

   a. "Hard" scientists could contribute significantly to our national ability toward hot or cold wars.
   b. "Soft" scientists also could contribute to waging hot and cold wars.

4. Average Americans were reinforced in the belief that, given opportunities and means, they could perform to the best of their individual abilities and succeed.

   a. Men had learned to wage war. War provided them firsthand experience in terms of leadership, organizational demands, human constraints, the limits of stress, and crisis response.
   b. Women could effectively replace men in war factories.

5. American basic industries were given unprecedented market opportunities domestically and internationally. Their competition internationally was minimal, and pent-up domestic demands were legion.

6. Pre-World War II scientists and engineers transferred back to their civilian positions to develop and produce nonwar consumer and industrial products.

7. The World War II young "hard" scientists and engineers working in wartime projects saw a continuing need for their dedicated services as well as lifetime careers devoted to developing the necessary R&D for national security and eventually space exploration.

The decade of the 1940s ended with an overpowering sense that America could police the world for the good of all nations and could build a domestic economy that would raise the average standard of living for all Americans.

It was easy in the immediate post–1945 era to get caught up in what you were doing especially if you were correcting the issues and concerns of the near past—namely, the Great Depression.

Basic industry in the 1950s was putting people to work and achieving employment levels wherein a 4 percent unemployment rate was considered as high. Increased emphasis on individual worker security was directly related to ever-expanding social security benefit laws, workmen's compensation packages, and private corporate health and pension plans.

All things considered, business and government in the 1950s did better than their predecessors of the 1920s and 1930s. They not only had provided higher employment, raised wages, and increased stock dividends, but also established the United States as a military, economic, and political power unprecedented in degree. At the same time, promising managers in high technology forged our nation's leadership in science and its commercialization and helped to establish the United States as a remarkable technological power.

The 1950s was a great decade for the American ego, because America was the envy of the world. It was such a heady time that it seemed unnecessary to measure the state of our society. Solutions to problems appeared simpler. If there were domestic or local economic troubles, one only had to wait four years for a new political party to be voted into power to apply the appropriate remedies.

There was no need to worry about regional economics. Trickle down effects from monetary, fiscal, and income policies worked in plenty of time. There was little need for industry to be concerned with crisis management or strategic planning. Growth made extrapolations of sales and earnings a reality. The stock markets reinforced managerial abilities and revealed performance at common stock multiple levels that had not been seen since the 1890s.

If the times were good, what were America's fears? Politically, the major fear was of communism at home and abroad. Economically, the only fear was whether we could provide enough human resources to meet expanding basic and technological markets. Shortages of capital or natural resources were at best secondary concerns. Wall Street was conditioned to provide annual equity capital for private sector growth. Its financial institutions, along with pension funds and insurance companies, helped finance governmental and private sector needs with long-term debt at reasonable interest rates; e.g., real rates ranged between -2 percent and +2 percent. Despite some fears, confidence in all institutions was extremely high by the end of the decade.

The 1960s was a decade of divisiveness. Trust in all our institutions declined as traditional ideals that had held us together as a nation were challenged. The cohesiveness of our nation was shattered by events. But even in the midst of these turbulent times, three key American perceptions were reinforced:

1. All people were equal under the law.
2. American abundance was limitless for foreign and domestic needs.
3. The nation was viewed as a leader in terms of marketing and communications.

In retrospect, we can see that a significant number of benefits emerged from this period in American history. By the end of the 1960s, colleges were the necessary means for the pursuit of a career beyond the blue collar or clerical work force. In 1968, the 6.9 million college students represented, for example, three times the number of farmers and nine times the number of railway workers. They formed a viable political force that could and did play major roles in terms of campus reform, political parties, campaign reforms and national issues such as Vietnam.

By the end of the decade, active women's movements had changed the role of women in American society. The role of Congress had also changed dramatically. The 88th and 89th Congresses dramatically altered the legal, social, and civil aspects of our society more than any other Congresses since the Civil War and the Great Depression.

The course of the Great Society was so charted that national administrations and political parties since have faced a number of problems. First, because each social program is deemed virtuous, reducing, altering, or eliminating it is difficult. The difficulty is compounded by the fact that each program has its own participative constituency that is skilled in the use of information technology. Second, entitlement programs have grown in cost, generally by several orders of magnitude more than originally estimated, while overall income has experienced limited growth. Moreover, all reform programs establish a permanent bureaucracy. Finally, American business as a whole in the 1960s and early 70s reacted with surprise to the social, political, and cultural changes. It took managers some time to realize what changes were taking place and then to regroup and reestablish new goals for their respective corporations and industries.

During the 1970s, the international position of the United States changed. The early 70s saw the impact of the revitalization of Europe and Asia. The first indications were that the dollar as a standard could not endure. Until then, the United States had held the financial world stable. As the other nations thrived, they surpassed the United States in selected technologies as well as in cheaper production and better quality of basic manufacturing goods. While we provided defense to our major competitors (West Germany and Japan), they concentrated on their own economic renewal. Thus they came into direct trade competition with the United States. While we converted many of our national resources, commodities, and supplies into defense goods, they used many of the same for trade goods. The emerging competition by highly industrialized nations for strategic security and economic resources became clearly evident by 1974 under double-digit inflation and cartel pricing of oil by the Organization of Petroleum Exporting Countries.

The state of the American society was heavily transfixed through international trade and political alliances. For the first time since 1890, the United States encountered an unfavorable balance of trade. This resulted in a run on the dollar at home and the building up of dollar reserves overseas to such an extent that the financing of American industry has been changed for decades to come.

The 1970s also witnessed the increasing parity between U.S. and USSR defense postures. The cold war was transformed into an uneasy and at times shaky détente with emphasis on arms limitation conferences. Providing both guns and butter was no longer a viable national economic policy. The financial interconnections between security requirements, entitlements, other governmental programs, balance of trade and private sector needs were complex and sometimes contradictory. For the first time in our history, we had stagflation—increased prices with increased unemployment. American business entities found themselves in competition with the government sector for equity funds as well as for working and fixed capital financing. The practical result was that venture capital dried up for most of the decade. Growth of small business firms with fewer than 20 employees including franchises became the major growth area for employment through the decade.

Today's young Americans have a new phenomenon to discuss with their future grandchildren; namely, the Great Inflation of the 1970s and 1980s. Federal deficits for the 1950s were $15 billion; in the 1960s, they increased more than fourfold to $63 billion; during the 1970s, the deficit of the 1950s was multiplied more than 25-fold or $420 billion. The Reagan administration is forecasting a deficit of over $420 billion for the fiscal period 1982–1984 alone. Both Democratic and Republican administrations have added to these ever-increasing deficits.

Tomorrow's prospectives for American society will be driven by both ideology and the resources at its disposal. Five assertions about these drivers are important.

1. There is a need for a public discussion, dissemination and acceptance of ideals.
2. There is a need to understand what resources are available to a society in order to redress its errors and develop its desired futures.
3. The differentiation of needed resources is essential for measuring the effectiveness of their usage for societal goals.
4. Resources, be they natural, human, or technological, are not yet considered as economic wealth or income ready for distribution. This distinction creates short-term discontinuities.
5. Creativity and innovation are the key ingredients for the next decade to resolve the problems facing American society. This creativity and innovation needs to be in science, technology, and management as well as in all our social and political processes.

RESEARCH AND DEVELOPMENT IN THE UNITED STATES

The decade of the 1960s brought about a significant shift in R&D expenditures in the United States. Figure 4-1 shows that the turning point for all R&D occurred in 1968. Decisionmakers in defense and space activities knew an era was ending several years prior to that. Rates of R&D expenditures changed to meet emerging national ideals of equality, abundance, and national markets. Defense R&D was reduced, while R&D for social goals such as health, environment and education was increased.

The 1968 level of defense R&D will not return until 1984. Let us not forget that commercialization is like a chain reaction. The catalyst of national defense and space R&D, when coupled with innovative World War II scientists and engineers and then joined with inventors and entrepreneurs of the 1950s and 1960s, resulted in the commercialization of advances for DOD and space projects in such

Figure 4-1. Total R&D Expenditures, 1960–1983, in Current Dollars and Constant Dollars (*1972 = 100 percent*).

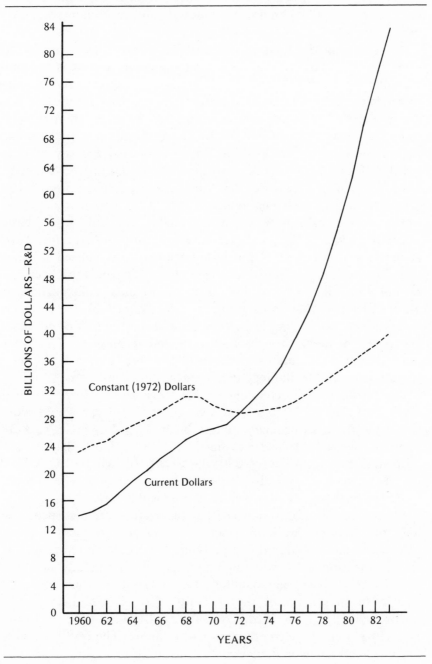

diverse areas as radar, electronics, computers, and operational and managerial research. This dynamic process brought the United States both scientific and technological leadership and ensured international prestige.

Transforming the Fourth Industrial Revolution cluster of innovations into the marketplace is a complex phenomenon. It is not simply adapting a technology to production of a product or service. The technologies are so numerous and interrelated that integration is a key element. The better one can integrate these in commercialization, the more effective will be the chain reaction and the stronger the competitive market position. Japan's national strategy has targeted technologies to specific markets by establishing government, university, and private sector development centers. The United States does not yet have such a national strategy.

U.S. tactics have been to institutionalize the bulk of its basic research in universities, colleges, and nonprofit institutions. Most applied research and development has been institutionalized in industry. Commercialization to meet new market demands has been left to individual institutions, with little or no cross-pollenization of ideas and techniques. As a result, a critical dimension for commercialization today is simply keeping up with the myriad of advances and potential breakthroughs in science and technology. This is far more than what we used to refer to as the "information explosion;" it is a science and technology (S&T) integration explosion.

Our scientific and technological knowledge base has been doubling every 10 years. In 1910 a week's worth of knowledge would probably have fit in an ordinary filing cabinet, $1' \times 1' \times 5'$ in size. By 1960 the weekly file had expanded to $1' \times 5' \times 60'$. It has been estimated that by the year 2000, the weekly file will be $15' \times 5' \times 60'$. Keeping up with all of this technological knowledge and advances in basic science may well be an impossible task.

Studies in the 1960s showed that the average chemist spent one hour per working day looking up data, four hours per day reading, and three hours per day doing productive work. Research to handle the information explosion required $1.5 billion annually in 1960, used to mechanize data handling and retrieval. If there were no changes in the system, by the year 2000 the cost would rise to $24 billion annually (in 1960 dollars). Today, DOD spends over $5 billion 1983 dollars on computer software alone. The results of such retrieval methods would give our chemist only an additional 45 minutes either to read or to do productive work. This is an unacceptable situation.

There are two other unacceptable alternatives: to do as little as possible to enjoy the affluent life or to work oneself into an early grave striving to keep up. Little research and development have been directed toward handling the S&T integration explosion in the U.S. until recently. Fortunately, there are now some beginnings in the private sector, by the Microelectronics and Computer Technology Corporation led by Admiral Bobby Inman, to tackle this problem. This must become a high priority for the United States if we are to meet and overcome the Japanese fifth generation computer, which threatens to supersede U.S. computer preeminence.

What is of more concern is the forthcoming international competition in science and economics. By the year 2000 this competition will be fierce. For example, National Science Foundation studies show that in 1960 the U.S. and Europe an educational structure produced 60 percent more university and college graduates than the rest of the world. If current trends continue, by the year 2000, Western domination will be reduced to 20 percent, and the Asian and Japanese graduates will increase significantly. This long-term situation cannot be ignored if we intend to maintain technological leadership and compete successfully in international trade. Today, NSF's projections are too close to reality for comfort.

To meet these challenges, R&D for the 1980s must take place within new institutional arrangements. More cooperative involvement is necessary between those institutions that perform basic research, those that do applied and developmental research, and those that are the sources of R&D funding. Emerging cooperative networks can do more than better disseminate the exploding body of knowledge. They can help resolve problems that arise from more stringent national security requirements and from growing pressures for international trade protection. Better yet, these institutional arrangements, by permitting more flexibility and adaptability in assessing research and technology, can assist in meeting the nation's needs in resolving rapidly changing security, economic, and political issues.

To understand better what may be involved in structurally transforming the U.S. economy, we need to examine R&D funding from several perspectives. The major source (over 50 percent) of total R&D funds in the decade of the 1960s was the federal government. However, by the end of the 1970s, industry R&D funds surpassed those of the federal government. The performance of most R&D has been and continues to be done by industry.

The federal government is still, by all measures, the major source for basic research. The performance of basic research before World War II was by industry and government laboratories. Since the 1960s, basic research has been primarily conducted by universities and colleges. Applied research and development research are predominantly performed by industry.

Federal R&D investment, by functions, for the decades of the 1960s and 1970s was predominantly for national defense and space research and technology. However, the relative growth of federal budget functions for R&D between 1971 and 1980 was as follows:

	Growth (%) 1971–1980
Energy	560
Health	200
Education	150
General science	140
Natural resources	125
Agriculture	100

In comparison, national defense and space research and technology rates of growth for the 1970s were only 65 percent and 53 percent, respectively. In many respects, Congress did reflect the American ideals of the 1960s and 1970s.

The national defense budget for 1983–1986, however, indicates a shift in the direction of funds. DOD expenditures between 1982 and 1986 will grow by 70 percent; expenditures for general science and basic research will rise by 33 percent; funds for space research, health, and education will all be decreased.

More revealing of R&D activities in the U.S. is the direct and strong correlation between federal spending, selected universities, geographic areas, and primary companies:

1. Basic research is generally conducted by less than 20 preeminent universities in California, New York, Massachusetts, Maryland, and the Washington, D.C. area.
2. In 1981 over 81 percent of the DOD research was invested in 15 states; 44 percent was in three states—California, Maryland, and Massachusetts, in that order.

3. New high-technology, nondefense companies tend to cluster in the same states where federal R&D funds are invested, namely California, Massachusetts, and New York. Maryland seems to be an exception to the rule.
4. DOD applied research and development research are conducted primarily by less than 20 companies, generally in the same states where federal R&D is conducted.

Between 1969 and 1980, industry R&D investments were predominantly in the high-technology and service sectors. The relative growth for this period by industry sectors was as follows:

	Growth (%) 1969–1980
Service	300
High technology	200
Basic industries	117

Within the basic industries sector, the relative growth was as follows:

	Growth (%) 1969–1980
Petroleum refining	232
Paper and allied products	168
Primary metals	165
Stone, clay and glass products	150
Rubber	150
Fabricated metal products	117

Relative growth in the high-technology sector was as follows:

	Growth (%) 1969–1980
Machinery	294
Professional and scientific instruments	207
Electrical equipment	110

The service industry's relative growth was 136 percent.

COMMERCIALIZATION OF TECHNOLOGY
RESOURCES FOR THE FUTURE

Figure 4-2 shows that commercialization consists of inputs as total R&D investments over time; transformation by sectors—that is, those who performed the R&D and outputs in terms of shipments, employment, and international balance of trade.

According to Figure 4-3, R&D inputs by industry were $19.5 billion for 1972 and $43.6 billion for 1980. This resulted directly or indirectly in increased manufactured shipments of $744 billion in 1972 and $1,851 billion in 1980. Figure 4-3 also shows that relative growth rates of shipments and R&D investments by sector roughly corresponded.

Total manufacturing employment rose slightly from 1972 to 1980. Figure 4-4 indicates that manufacturing employment increased more for high-technology industries than for basic and other manufacturing industries. During the same period, scientific and engineering employment increased significantly, as shows in Figure 4-5. Thus, as R&D investments increase in high-technology industries,

Figure 4-2. Commercialization Process.

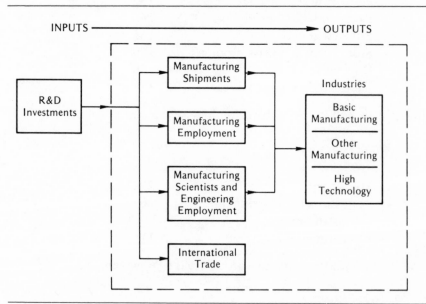

Figure 4-3. Commercialization Process: R&D Investment and Manufacturing Shipments, 1972 and 1980.

R&D Processors	R&D Investments (Billion $)				Manufacturing Shipments (Billion $)		
	1972	1980	Percentage Increase (1980/1972)		1972	1980	Percentage Increase (1980/1972)
Total	$19.5	$43.6	121	→	$744.0	$1,851.0	149
Basic industry	1.8	4.3	139		298.2	766.9	157
Other manufacturing	.5	1.1	120		225.2	487.4	116
High technology	16.6	36.7	121		221.0	596.7	170
Services	.7	1.6	129		N/A	N/A	N/A

INPUTS ―――――――――――――――――――► OUTPUTS

Figure 4-4. Commercialization Process: R&D Investment and Manufacturing Employment, 1972 and 1980.

R&D Processors	R&D Investments (Billion $)				Total Manufacturing Employment (Millions)		
	1972	1980	Percentage Increase (1980/1972)		1972	1980	Percentage Increase (1980/1972)
Total	$19.5	$43.6	121	→	19.1	20.3	+6
Basic industry	1.8	4.3	139		7.0	6.9	−1
Other manufacturing	.5	1.1	120		6.3	6.2	−2
High technology	16.6	36.7	121		5.8	7.2	+24
Services	.7	1.6	129		N/A	N/A	N/A

INPUTS ―――――――――――――――――――► OUTPUTS

Figure 4-5. Commercialization Process: R&D Investment and Full-Time Employment of Scientists and Engineers, 1972 and 1980.

R&D Processors	R&D Investments (Billion $)				Full-Time-Equivalent Number R&D Scientists and Engineers (Thousands)		
	1972	1980	Percentage Increase (1980/1972)		1972	1980	Percentage Increase (1980/1972)
Total	$19.5	$43.6	121	➤	354.0[a]	458.4[a]	29
Basic industry	1.8	4.3	139		38.8	51.5	33
Other manufacturing	.5	1.1	120		11.9	14.1	18
High technology	16.6	36.7	121		284.0	361.2	27
Services	.7	1.6	129		15.7	18.9	20

INPUTS ——————————————————————————➤ OUTPUTS

a. Rounding errors.

there seems to be a reduced demand for blue collar workers. In fact, the highest relative growth for scientists and engineers occurred in basic industries.

Figures 4-6 and 4-7 show that between 1974 and 1979 the United States lost its relative position in imports and exports of both high- and low-technology manufacturing.

Clearly, we must improve each of the three aspects of the commercialization process to expand employment and to strengthen our international trading position.

Using constant 1972 dollars, defense expenditures in 1979 are estimated to amount to 21 percent. Table 4-1 shows the relative increase is more in the basic industries than high technology. On the other hand, defense expenditures in high-technology manufacturing are over five times as much as basic industry shipments.

To promote the commercialization process while ensuring our national security, the private sector must work more harmoniously with state and federal governments. Together they must address problems and opportunities in four major areas: the challenge of competition, the cartelization of R&D, incentives for technological development, and measures for productivity.

Figure 4-6. Change in High-Technology Market Shares, 1974–1979.

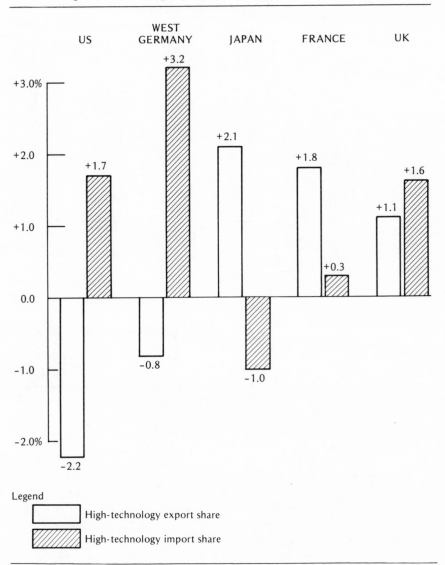

Figure 4–7. Change in Low-Technology Market Shares, 1974–1979.

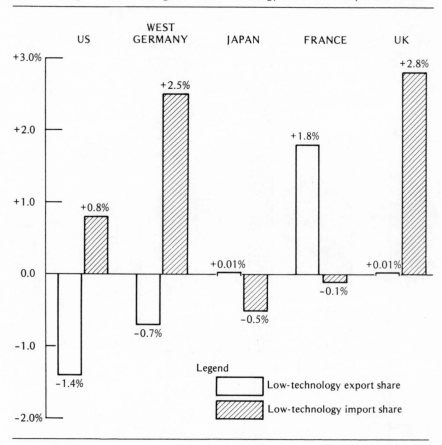

Table 4-1. Value of 1979 and 1985 Manufacturing Shipments by Industry, Defense Expenditures, and Percentage of Total Manufacturing Shipments (*Million 1972 $*).

	1979		1985	
Sector	*Defense Expenditures*	*Percentage*	*Defense Expenditures*	*Percentage*
Basic industry	$ 6,092	8	$ 9,802	12
Other manufacturing	38	12	58	15
High technology	29,772	21	53,399	27
Services	2,132	7	2,954	8

5 THE IMPACT OF TECHNOLOGY ON DECISIONMAKING

The impact of technology on decisionmaking will always depend on the ability to link human and technological resources in the decisionmaking activities. This linkage provides a way to deepen our scientific and practical understanding of the process by which these resources are developed, allocated, and utilized.

For the next decade we will be involved with important issues that face the managements of for-profit as well as not-for-profit institutions. Technology will have a definite impact on managerial decisionmaking processes. How much of an impact will depend on how well the linkages are structured among those who formulate the decision problems for solution, those who model the problems for specified telecommunication systems, those managers who make the decisions, and finally those who assess the accountability of the decisionmakers. These linkages were not required before, but their significance is essential now in order to adapt new concepts that technologies have made possible. This chapter is concerned with the current state of decision technology and the impacts of future information technology developments on decisionmaking.

CURRENT STATE OF DECISION TECHNOLOGY

Today, there is a dichotomy in the evolution of developments in and applications of decision technology. Too often problem formulators are working on predicting problems of the future without reference to present realities or available resources to actualize their predictions. Too often managers are working on current problems without considering the consequences of their actions on the future. And this, perhaps, is the major point: Important choices lie before us, but they cannot be made in a monolithic way. Decision technologists, managers, users, and assessors are, in an era of critical experimentation, trying to find the "best way." There is probably no best way at all—only better ways for a while, for different groups, different areas. But we are well advised to observe closely what we are about and what results from what we do.

The management of change becomes the management of the creation and application of information technology that will enable individual institutions to achieve their goals. Policymaking centers are innovative concepts in developing the context for the management of change.

Once policy is seen as an intention to affect or direct the future in a specified manner, and policymaking centers are identified as those institutions or organizations that have the ability to affect the future, developments in decision and information technology are the results of policy setting and subsequent action on the part of policymaking institutions. It should be noted that in concentrating on *policy* centers, the focus is on the *context* for decisionmaking rather than on the *operations* associated with the production of goods and services. That is, the emphasis is on the role of top management rather than on the activities of lower level managers.

Information technology provides business policymaking centers an opportunity to design, modify, or add relevant industries, companies, and other entities in the utilization and allocation of society's scarce resources to its constituents. It is not possible to identify clearly specific classes of business policymaking centers in the United States. Perhaps there has been no reason to structure any hierarchy of business policymaking centers. Furthermore, all of our socioeconomic mores suggest that society does not need these centers, does not want them, and should not have them.

However, perceptions of some order with regard to U.S. business have been generally held. Most people have an image of business as being a set of clusters of corporations, people, and buildings identified with and identifiable by the goods and services they produce. Those outside of the clusters often perceive them as monolithic interest groups. In some cases it has become convenient for those within the clusters to adopt a similar perception. In other cases those who formed a cluster adopted an identification as an interest group to promote their image or to enhance the adoption of their policies.

Businesses and business leaders are associated with organizations ranging from trade associations, to chambers of commerce, to other business/social clubs. In no formal way are such associations policy-making centers in the sense that they set policy for the nation. Yet in many respects they are still viable and influential organizations within our current theory of political democracy.

Policymaking clusters within business can, therefore, be an image generated for convenience of communication, or to make a point, as well as of actual makers of policy. For example, the need for private personal transportation led to the development of the automobile. The development of a personalized vehicle has created an automotive cluster that employs 1 of every 6 Americans. Within the cluster are automobile and parts manufacturers and distributors; service and maintenance entities; the oil industry; steel, glass, paint, textiles, rubber, and insurance companies; and other important private suppliers of goods and services. Other classes of business clusters, such as highway construction, hotels and motels, and recreational areas have also appended themselves to the growth of the "automotive clusters." These clusters in turn affect other policymaking centers within the governmental and educational policy centers. It is possible, in many respects, to view clusters as following a mitotic natural process, much along the line of cells splitting into other cells. However, by their association with different industries and services as well as governmental entities, we can see a shift of policymaking from one type of cluster (e.g., automobile production) to another cluster even outside of business (e.g., the federal government). In this respect policymaking centers are not static but dynamic and one needs to be able to assemble information that identifies the policymaking locus over time. At best, information technology may serve to identify a series of centers that somehow combine to make policy decisions that affect society.

Decision Technology Process

This section sets forth an analysis of how the formulation, use, and assessment of the decision process takes place in the development of

Table 5-1. Schema of the Formulation, Development, Use, and Assessment of Decision Technology.

Activity	Output	Human Resources
Formulation	New knowledge and theory	Scholars
Modelling	Testing and extending the formulation of new knowledge and theory	Applied management scholars
Decision Making	Decision based on new knowledge and theory	Chief executive officers and other managers
Assessment	Evaluation for effectiveness and efficiency of the outputs	Auditors for legal, engineering, managerial, and financial decision functions (internal and external)

decision technology. It is important that we understand this currently loose process in order to gain the most from the process and assess the impact of present and future information technologies in the decision processes. Too often the issues and problems that need solution are not communicated to the theoretical management scholar. Often the intellectual power is not focused on the more critical areas of institutional concern.

Table 5-1 identifies the activities in decision technologies as well as their output and their skilled human resources. Several important points are made in the table.

1. The activities have produced important outputs including new theories and techniques that have led to real improvements in decisionmaking.

2. The advances to date have been unlinked. Each group, be they the theoretical builders (problem formulators and modelers), the users (decisionmakers), or auditors (assessment) have not really been coordinated with the decisionmaking process. Probably less than 5 percent of all the new ideas in the composite activities expressed or published are understood or used.

3. The need for linkage of the decision technology has never been a primary concern of management schools, managers, or auditors.

4. The issues fundamental to the national welfare as well as emerging information technology make it virtually certain that the linkage will be the next major frontier for all involved in decision technology activities.

Let me present an example in which I was personally involved in the analysis of "cause and effect"—the National Commission on Supplies and Shortages. The Commission's report stated:

> The shortages of 1973–74 [other than oil] were not caused by an insufficiency of world resources, but by the combined effects of a slowdown in the growth of productive capacity, a sharp increase in demand that occurred virtually simultaneously in most industrialized countries, and a "shortage mentality" under which private inventories were built up to excessive levels. Our commodity studies and other evidence demonstrate that the Government did not fully grasp the implications of those events as they developed; that its actions contributed to their development; and that the steps taken to alleviate the shortages were, at best, only marginally effective and, at worst, counterproductive. We believe that the inadequacy of the Government's materials and (to a much smaller degree) food information systems contributed to this failure.

The Commission recommended the following improvements in government's data and analysis.

- Data must be made more accurate, complete, explicit, and objective.
- Better early warning of impeding problems must be developed.
- The relationship between information and policy action must be strengthened.
- An integrated overview of food and materials issues must be developed.
- A better understanding of the relationships between commodities, energy, and the environment must be fostered.

Finally, the following 10 guidelines were recommended.

1. Data collection and data analysis should be organizationally separate from policy and program activities.
2. Data collection and data analysis should be placed in separate, high-level (preferably bureau level) organizations of comparable status.

3. The credibility of data and analysis should be maintained through open access, advisory committees, and other institutional safeguards.
4. Data collection and analysis should be responsive to the needs of users.
5. Statistical standards should be upgraded, and the limitations of the data—including sampling error, uncertainty, and assumption—should be published with the data.
6. Policy analysis should be separated from data collection and data analysis and from programmatic and promotional responsibilities.
7. Policy analysis should be encouraged at various levels within line departments.
8. Policy analyses should be made public when possible.
9. All policy analysts should work from comparable and consistent data.
10. A primary responsibility of higher level policy analysts should be to reconcile conflicting analyses.

In business little analysis is done to establish a firm's data collection and analysis for its decisionmaking that links data collection, analysis, policy analysis, and policymaking. Certainly variables of most business decision models are not linked to the chart of accounts in order to convert them from planning models into control models.

IMPACT OF DECISION TECHNOLOGY

The first issue that confronts today's managers is whether they are to approach the future on the basis of choice or on the basis of prediction. If the issue is resolved in favor of prediction, then we have left the future in the hands of the problem formulators without providing any assurance that the insights they may develop will ever be acted upon. On the other hand, if the issue is resolved in favor of choice, we have left the future in the hands of the managers without any guarantee that their solutions will be directed toward the anticipated problems of its institutions or society.

The point is that this issue and all of the issues that follow are not *either/or* decisions; rather they can be *both/and* decisions. Rather than choose either prediction or choice, we can select a system in which both choice and prediction play a role.

Management scholars in a large number of academic institutions, professional groups, and corporate laboratories are currently engaged in developing new operations research techniques, new computer algorithms, and new models directed toward solving important classes of problems. Many of these classes of problems, such as inventory control, scheduling, forecasting, activity sequencing, and capital budgeting have been addressed by management scholars for the past 30 years or so.

Also emerging, however, are new classes of management planning and control decision problems to be investigated by management scholars and scientists.[1] Some of the characteristics of these problems are as follows.

1. The problems involve more than one level of management.
2. They involve highly complex and diversified activities.
3. They deal more with service processes.
4. They involve interrelationships between economic, social, and cultural objectives of individuals and institutions.
5. They require the handling of great volumes of data.
6. The time frame for the solution of these classes of problems is compressed.
7. The effects of possible alternative solutions are far-reaching in terms of both timing of impact and number of individuals affected.

Any attempt to address these new classes of problems must go beyond merely developing new techniques, algorithms, or models or simply searching for new applications of existing tools. These new problems require that we develop new conceptual constructs that will extend the capabilities of their discipline across a broad front and along many dimensions as well as call for a new order of information technology capacity.

Conceptual constructs for the application of management decision models have not, as a rule, been in the forefront of management scholars' considerations. They rarely appear in the current literature in explicit fashion—if they are present at all. Yet, such constructs are implicit in the presentations of both theory and applications and by inference they may be made more explicit.

Before heading further into the impact that technology has had and will have on the decision process, it is important to examine the managerial aspects of the decision process. This involves the spectrum of decision processes relative to the manner of organizations, the style of management, what parameters are needed to consider the managerial aspects, and how these parameters are interrelated with the financial decision processes. The finance literature has not generally agreed upon theory or delineated managerial parameters regarding investment management. The managerial literature has yet to include a combination of financial theory for investments with management decision theory. The relevant concepts that do exist in the managerial literature are fragmented and embodied in the various traditional categories of management literature.

There is a need to delineate the more applicable management principles, theories, practices, and logic found through a select survey of broad managerial literature areas—a management epistemology. This is necessary in order to identify critical and applicable management principles and practices with problems of investment and decision support in order to link the decision technology processes.

Figure 5-1 presents the conceptual management decision epistemology used in the aforementioned investment problem. In this figure it is assumed that managerial epistemology can be illustrated as a wheel. The hub contains the critical managerial parameters. Radiating from the hub are a series of spokes that delineate at the rim the vectors of management epistemology. The vectors are taken from a series of academic disciplines and in turn can be broken down to include primary theories and techniques related to the disciplines. These techniques and theories are classified by critical parameters rather than being compiled by specific elements of knowledge.

Note further that there are six disciplines specifically selected:

1. Managerial organization theories
2. Management planning and control frameworks
3. Management decision support
4. Management reports
5. Management styles
6. Mathematical model parameters

It is not claimed that these areas represent all applicable management epistemology in the extension of management theory to investment decisionmaking. These specific management epistemological areas are selected on the basis of relevance and contribution to the design of decision support systems in investment management and as such are not intended as an exhaustive review of the literature.

Figure 5-1. Management Epistemology.

Decision management for formulators and modelers has yet to have its own well-defined epistemology. It is still fragmented; its techniques are piecemeal. And techniques are often found within various business functions and even outside the study of business; e.g., economics, psychology, sociology, mathematics, computer sciences, control and feedback engineering, and production control.

In many instances the literature overlaps theories and disciplines. In fact, in some cases the exact same words and phrases take on quite different meanings and imply different concepts when traversing the various disciplines. But here the theoretical overlaps and ambiguities will not be resolved, although they do affect the use and application of technology and its promise for a better day for the decisionmaker.

It is possible to add to the management decisionmaking epistemology the various aspects of portfolio theory, namely risk-return model, index model, capital asset pricing model, and state preference model. It is now possible to delineate the theory and modeling used for an interlinked model for investment firm management policy and operational decisionmaking. Table 5–2 shows the summary details. The conceptual construct that was computerized is shown in Figure 5–2. This chapter is not the place for details on policymaking, establishment of goals, strategy, and policy constraints coupled with operations rules and organizational responsibilities.[2] The major point is that we recognize the capacity to link formulation, modeling, testing and evaluation, managerial strategy, and operations with assessment using current theory and information technology.

To date, no systems theory has been developed to encompass all aspects of financial decision management. It is important that we continue to work on theory and application techniques and develop strong decision support systems. However, it is more important for us to realize that currently we have decisions to make that require better utilization of current knowledge and technology. Information and analysis using existing theories and techniques are underutilized and can make a contribution to the decision processes. They require an appropriate epistemology, technology, and training so that their values can be appreciated.

Table 5-2.   Management Epistemology: A Comparison of the Models of Eisuu and the IIM Model.

Management Epistemology	Survey of the Literature	Portfolio Theory Model	IIM Model
Management organization theories	Economic theory of the firm Behavioral theory of the firm Information theory of the firm	Economic theory of the firm	Economic theory of the firm Behavioral theory of the firm Information theory of the firm
Management planning and control frameworks	Charnes and Cooper: Planning-operation-control Anthony: Managerial control—operational control Japanese: System of corporate management and planning	None	Charnes and Cooper: Planning-operation-control Anthony: Managerial control—operational control Japanese: System of corporate management and planning
Management decision design	Management by exception Management by predictive acceptance	Management by predictive acceptance	Management by exception Management by predictive acceptance
Management reports	Purpose: Scorecard; attention-getting; problem-solving; decisionmaking Type: Feedback; feed-forward	Problem-solving Decisionmaking Feed-forward	Scorecard; attention-getting; problem-solving; decision-making Feedback; feed-forward
Management styles	Professional; entrepreneurial; adaptive	Professional	Adaptive
Mathematical model parameters	Objective function: Optimization; satisficing Class of models; replacement; augmentation; shadowing	Optimization Replacement	Satisficing Shadowing

Figure 5–2. Revised Conceptualized Decision Processes.

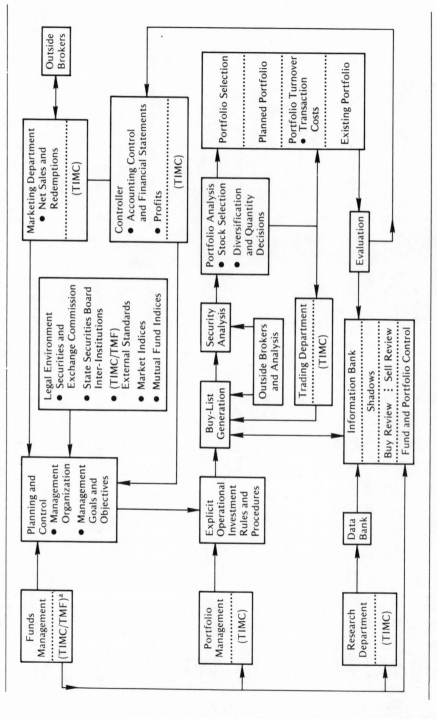

a. TIMC = The Investment Management Corporation; TMF = The Mutual Fund Corporation.

IMPACT OF FUTURE INFORMATION
TECHNOLOGY ON DECISIONMAKING

In this section we shall look into advances in the technologies of computers and communications linked to knowledge processing and decision support systems. The computer complex for the 1990s will overcome many of the problems in today's decision systems. Simply stated, these problems are

1. Computers were designed primarily for numerical computation and not for business decision processing.
2. The cost of hardware required a performance ratio that put emphasis on speed of central processing and larger memories.
3. The cost of developing software has gradually increased to where it is almost ineffective to organize and maintain.
4. Communications has not been effectively integrated with computers.

Today's managerial decision processes are limited. Future managerial decision processes require

1. More knowledge about what is available and feasible rather than what is the current data on information bases
2. Conversation in natural language as opposed to current software language
3. The ability to retrieve and use decision models with associative knowledge, data, and information bases including error analysis as well as the ability to retrieve and use pictorial and image data
4. The ability to compress data for decisionmaking in order to generate better alternatives.

As we move toward the 1990s, we will need to become a knowledge processing society rather than a data processing society. In our highly developed technological society, there are no longer any simple problems or issues. Even the design, manufacture, marketing, and sale of a toy to bring a child joy produces a series of management decisions requiring the most sophisticated knowledge data bases and analysis techniques in order to assess the risk and rewards associated with this task.

It is now fortunate that in many parts of the world what the Japanese call the "fifth generation computers" are developing. These information processing techniques will resolve today's problems with information technology for decision processes. It will be a period of change in internal and external conditions and the timely analysis, processing, and display of pertinent knowledge, data and information will be essential.

What will be our future choices, frustrations, achievements, and setbacks as the management decision technology processes interact with various technologies and the unpredictable, creative impulse of the human spirit? As shown in Figure 5-1, the accounting function plays a major role in assessment. Accounting either as a discipline or a profession has not yet generally accepted the responsibility for legal, engineering, or managerial audit. Accounting as an academic discipline will evolve during the 1980s and 1990s as the assessor of these functions as it plays a more important role in the decisionmaking processes.

The assessment function will then become easier but far from simple as the knowledge technologies are developed. The advances of the fifth generation knowledge based computers will hasten the day when we will be able to push the frontiers of accounting and accept these functions. The audit of surrogates for decisionmaking will be enhanced through the new computer systems. Also, the ability to utilize and process all types of knowledge bases will permit assessors to measure the efficiency and effectiveness of the use of decision models for management decisions, compliance with legal and regulatory restrictions, and the utilization of advanced technology in the development of new products and services.

FIFTH GENERATION COMPUTERS

Let us now put into perspective the new generation of technology and innovation. Much material here is taken from a preliminary report on the study and research on the next generation of computer capability prepared by the Japan Information Processing Development Center. I have added my own analysis and opinions drawn from many years in knowledge data base design, computer hardware development, and management decision support research.

The new computer systems will be designed based on their ability to produce effective technology decision support. They must overcome the current technical limitations inherent in conventional computers. The 1990s system must retrieve appropriate programs from a knowledge base on the basis of the user requirements and then develop a program or decision criterion by inference. The system must be able to verify the program or decision criterion by inference. The system, after it has verified the program or decision criterion by inference, must then determine that the program generated meets the requirements in an optimal or satisfying manner.

Figure 5-3 is a conceptual diagram of a computer system that may give the power and flexibility required for better decision support. It includes modules that deal with

- Understanding of a problem's description and requirement specifications
- Synthesizing processing procedures
- Optimization between machine system and processing procedures
- Synthesizing response based on outputs from the machine system
- Intelligent interface functions capable of understanding speech, image, display, natural language

There must be, of course, knowledge data bases that support all of the desired functions. The knowledge data base contains accumulated, valid, and universal knowledge necessary to the user. This base will have three types of data.

1. General knowledge base that mainly relates to the understanding of natural languages
2. The knowledge base related to the system
3. Applied knowledge base containing specified information for the specific application

A *knowledge base* is all material on a subject in a library as well as proprietary know-how, including current managerial operational rules and procedures. The 1990s system will have very friendly interfaces to be used for the human/machine, machine/human, and machine/machine communication. The language must be appropriate to the human's normal language and will include sensing other human inputs.

Figure 5-4 is a conceptual software configuration for the next generation computer systems. It consists of applications systems, basic application systems, intelligent utility systems, intelligent sys-

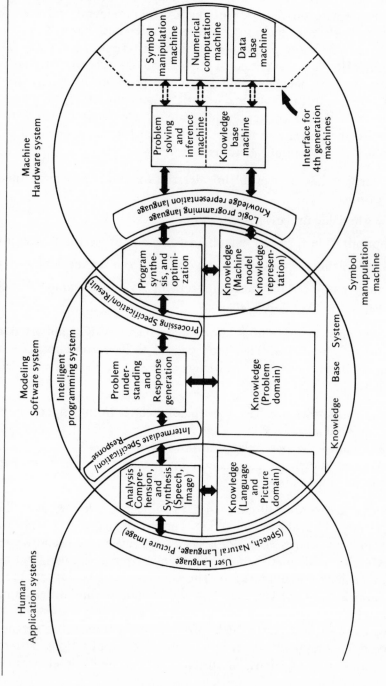

Figure 5-3. Conceptual Diagram of the Next Generation Computer Systems.

Source: Japan Information Processing Development Center.

Figure 5-4. Conceptual Diagram of the Next Generation Computer Software System.

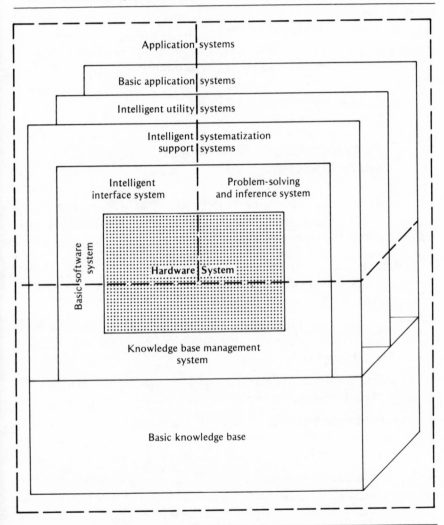

Source: Japan Information Processing Development Center.

tem support systems, basic software systems, the knowledge data base managerial system, basic knowledge data bases, an intelligent interface system, a problem-solving interface system—all working in harmony with the hardware system.

What will this system do for us? Among many things, it will allow us to ask questions and get answers. It will organize our knowledge for the decisions we want to make. The system will provide office automation, computer-aided design, engineering, and instruction. It will also offer applied speech understanding and applied problem solving. The impact on accounting of future technology including the fifth generation computers will be large.

FUTURE TECHNOLOGY IMPACT ON ACCOUNTING

The impact on the accounting profession of the new decision technologies will be many, but like all future potential will require preparation, courage, acceptance, and involvement.

- Distributed national and global networks with access to knowledge bases worldwide and intelligent friendly interfaces will increase the audit function and scope.

- Internal auditing will dramatically increase and will include measures of efficiency for the institution's data bases and decision model and support functions.

- Assessing nonfinancial activities of institutions will demand different knowledge bases, expertise, relationships, and training.

- The audit function will be extended to include measures of the efficiency and effectiveness of management beyond return on investment, liquidity, work unit efficiency, earnings per share.

- Firms can expect to get measures of effectiveness of current operations in meeting goals, technology transfer, and development and delivery of new products, goods, and services.

- Accounting firms will be able to broaden their services to all sizes of firms and institutions to include technology and venture assessment, effectiveness measures, internal audit.

- Accounting firms will be able to get into the knowledge processing and delivery business.

The impacts of technology offer potential solutions to many current problems, but their realization depends on how we link our human and technological resources. This is the time for innovation and action. It is now possible, and feasible, to link human and technological resources through the development of knowledge data bases and decision support systems. If American business doesn't act now, we will have forgone a rare opportunity to regain the technological lead as well as to advance the accounting profession, its management, education, and opportunity.

A graduate school of accounting within the framework of a graduate school of business in a university with outstanding computer and communications technology is the appropriate sphere for developing the decision support system theory and education. We educators need to redesign the education process to teach decision processes within the future support and technology reality. The graduate school of accounting must focus on teaching comprehensive audits or assessment principles and purpose. It needs to create an appropriate system for an evaluation that provides real accountability. In addition, the academic accounting community has the responsibility to do the coordination and research required in the development of an acceptable body of knowledge in the areas of financial, legal, engineering, and management assessment of decision support systems and their concomitant technology. The academic accounting community will require the necessary support of all accounting professions as well as of the managers of for-profit and not-for-profit institutions.

NOTES TO CHAPTER 5

1. Timothy Ruefli, "Extensions of Management Science," unpublished report, IC^2 Institute, The University of Texas at Austin.
2. Ray E. Whitmire, "Institutional Investment Management Model: Long-Term Goals, Strategy and Short-Term Adaptive Operations," doctoral dissertation, The University of Texas at Austin, December 1975.

6

IMPACT OF NATIONAL ECONOMIC INITIATIVES ON STEEL AND OTHER BASIC INDUSTRIES

This is a period of great uncertainty, domestically and internationally, for a number of American industries, especially the troubled steel industry. It is a particularly nerve-wracking period for many leaders in the public and private sectors. Most managers have had difficulties relying on past experience or drawing upon a theoretical framework applicable to today's environment for the economic recovery of their firms. This recovery will lead to times when there can be acceptable employment or unemployment rates, higher profits, accessible capital markets at fair rates, controllable inflation, a strong national security status, balanced international opportunities, an improved overall national research and development posture, and a reasonable quality of life.

This chapter concentrates on the fiscal, technological, and other national critical issues for subsequent formulation of national initiatives. The impacts of fiscal and other national policies must be viewed from an overall national perspective rather than just for a particular industry such as the steel industry. Steel is an important basic industry and is vital to the nation's security and prosperity. For two reasons, it is necessary to distinguish national policies addressing basic industries as contrasted to those focussing on high-technology industries and the service sector.

First, today's national economic uncertainties and managerial stresses will not disappear by simply expanding our high-technology industries. Second, the United States requires more than renewal or revitalization; it needs a viable agenda that structurally transforms its economy to more realistically utilize its resources and economic wealth to longer term national needs.

The steel industry requires transformation more than it needs renewal or restructuring to match current or short-term foreign competition. Catch-up is not the name of the game. Survival and leap-frog are the name of the game for the 1980s and 1990s.

Transformation of the steel industry comes from at least four major sources:

1. Very rapid and often wide swings in demand for steel products place more emphasis on availability while maintaining costs within competitive prices. Witness the U.S. need for tubular and pipe products for the energy industry during 1981–82. Just as added modern domestic facilities were being planned or built, the demand evaporated and caught everyone by surprise. The results were slowdowns and shutdowns. Many independents in the energy industry are still in shock.

2. Emerging new customer requirements for specialized products, better quality in terms of their own subsequent processing and the need for better distribution methods that reduce delivery times as well as working capital requirements. Specialty steel requirements are emerging in the newer fields of computerization, biotechnology, robotics, waste management, water distribution, telecommunications, and transportation, among others. These newer demands are in their precommercialization and preconsumer demand states and could have a definite bearing on highly specialized steel plants—on their size, technology, and location.

3. Increasing international and domestic competition for more efficiently produced steel requires constant injections of capital and vigorous financial marketing and better methods of distribution. The movement of industry to the Sunbelt states has yet to be taken into account in terms of improved transportation by rail and truck, and its public infrastructure. All of this places demands for transformation of the steel industry and for relevant national initiatives.

4. Continuous pressures for increased wage rates, associated benefits, and quality of work environment require the adoption of technological innovations and other mechanisms for increased productivity and products costs flexibility. This will lead to "de-skilling" the

labor content—better manpower management in the use of skilled help and upgrading of unskilled help. Equally important, these pressures will require innovative managerial methods for accomplishing the transformation of financing capital improvements as well as shortening the working capital cycles for both the steel industry and its customers. Pressure will increase to improve the productivity of general administration's marketing and selling functions. Steel's survival cannot be based on steel alone. Its major markets have been for some time the other basic industries, simultaneously facing the same critical problems. To solve one without dealing with the others is unrealistic. Steel cannot just look out for itself and expect favorable government policies to bail it out. Most of the nation's basic industries are in the same predicament, which makes it easier to discuss national initiatives.

The public, and in some respects investors, view most of the basic industries as poor and having shrinking markets, large overcapacities, and facing fierce competition with highly industrialized as well as developing nations. They believe that the basic industries require government intervention ranging from large subsidies to crises cartels, trigger prices, import quotas, tariff barriers, and the establishment of more efficient and effective foreign controlled plants domestically.

The following tables summarize how the basic industries, including steel, relate to high-technology industries, service industry and tobacco, food and kindred products in terms of manufactured shipments, employment and wage rates.

Table 6-1 shows that other basic industries have had a great impact on the steel industry because of steel's large market dependence on these basic industries.

Table 6-2 shows that manufacturing shipments are still made predominantly by basic industries. Although other selected dates and definitions of basic industries can be used, Table 6-3 shows that the national economy must continue to rely heavily on basic industries to catalyze progress and growth. High-technology industries, as defined by the Congressional Joint Economic Committee in its 1982 report, "Location of High Technology Firms and Regional Economic Development," have added no more than 3 percent in the past decade to the total manufacturers' shipments. The basic industries have been relatively stable at about 41 percent of the total manufacturers' shipments.

Table 6-1. Steel's Relations to Other Basic Industries (*in Terms of Markets*).

Other Basic Industries	Primary	Secondary	Tertiary
Motor vehicles and parts	X		
Primary metal industries	X		
Fabricated metal products	X		
Stone, clay, and glass products		X	
Textile mill products			X
Paper and allied products		X	
Petroleum and coal products	X	X	
Rubber and plastics products	X	X	

Table 6-4 shows that manufacturing employment in basic industries is significant: over 20 million workers. Employment has contracted under past national economic policies as well as corporate policies. Table 6-5 shows that doubling of high-technology shipments employment is not a realistic expectation, at least in the next decade. Therefore, high-technology expansion will not abrogate today's unemployment in the short term, nor is it a substitute for possible continued contraction in U.S. basic industries. We must continue to transform our basic industries, including steel, to provide employment opportunities at home and to expand exports.

Table 6-6 shows that the high-technology industries are not the high average labor rate industries. Table 6-7 shows that the average hourly wages for the basic industries were approximately 6 cents below the high-technology industries in 1972 but increased to 12 cents more in 1981. If we eliminate the textile mill products, the difference for the basic industries is higher by 59 cents. Steel hourly wage rates are still about $2 per hour higher than high-technology firms—a substantial difference considering that in 1972 the industries' average labor rates were about the same. Averages also mask the fact that many more workers are being paid over $20 per hour in the steel, automobile, and petroleum industries than in high-technology industries. Table 6-8 gives a synopsis of hourly rates in the basic industries, high-technology and other durable and nondurable goods fields for more clarity.

Trends indicating stable manufacturing shipments, slowly declining employment, and increasing wage rates for the basic industries

Table 6-2. Manufacturers' Shipments for Selected Periods (*Billion $*).[a]

	1972	1980	1981
Total Manufacturers' Shipments	*$744*	*$1,851*	*$1,995*
A. *Basic Industries*			
Motor vehicles and parts	$ 66.8	$104.6	$114.9
Primary metals	57.9	133.9	136.8
Fabricated metal products	47.1	116.2	123.3
Stone, clay, and glass products	22.3	46.1	49.1
Textile mill products	26.7	47.4	52.3
Paper and allied products	28.3	72.7	79.5
Petroleum and coal products	29.9	198.7	220.3
Rubber and plastics products	19.2	47.3	46.5
	$298.2	$766.9	$822.7
As a percentage of total shipments	40%	41%	41%
B. *High Technology*			
Machinery except electrical	$ 61.0	$180.7	$203.7
Electrical machinery	56.0	128.6	137.9
Transportation equipment except motor vehicles and parts	33.2	81.7	88.1
Instruments and related products	13.4	44.1	47.5
Chemicals and allied products	57.4	161.6	175.1
	$221.0	$596.7	$652.3
As a percentage of total shipments	30%	32%	33%
C. *Food and Kindred Products Including Tobacco*	$120.4	$267.8	$282.1
As a percentage of total shipments	16%	15%	14%
D. *Other Durable and Nondurable Goods*	$104.8	$219.6	$237.4
As a percentage of total shipments	14%	12%	12%

a. Not seasonally adjusted.
Source: Survey of Current Business.

Table 6-3. Manufacturers' Shipments for Selected Periods
(*as a Percentage of Total Manufacturers' Shipments*).[a]

	1972	1980	1981
A. Basic industries	40%	41%	41%
B. High technology	30%	32%	33%
C. Food and kindred products including tobacco	16%	15%	14%
D. Other durable and nondurable goods	14%	12%	12%

a. Not seasonally adjusted.

Table 6-4. Employment by Sectors for Selected Periods
(*in Millions*).[a]

	1972	1980	1981
Total Employees	73.7	90.4	91.1
Mining	.6	1.0	1.1
Construction	3.8	4.3	4.2
Manufacturing	19.1	20.3	20.2
Service-producing including government	50.2	64.7	65.6

a. Not seasonally adjusted.
Source: Survey of Current Business.

including steel are continuing. A May 1982 *Iron Age* article reported that "a major contraction in the industry seems to be underway. A new scenario is beginning to emerge with steel smaller, leaner and more profitable."[1] The same article reported an increase in steel imports and a decline of over a quarter of a million in domestic employment.

The questions that national policy initiatives should address are

1. Can the United States really afford to lose employment?
2. Shouldn't we boldly question contraction as a national economic initiative for basic industries as well as for steel?
3. Can we really blame the steel industry for dropping modernization and expansion plans for domestic steel that would have been a big step toward world-class supremacy?

When facing such unpleasant questions, theory and the best management practices often help to delineate the critical issues that lead

Table 6-5. Employment in Manufacturing for Selected Periods (*in Millions*).[a]

Manufacturing	1972	1980	1981
A. *Basic Industries*			
Motor vehicles and parts	$1.2	$1.1	$1.1
Primary metals	1.2	1.1	1.1
Fabricated metal products	1.4	1.6	1.6
Stone, clay, and glass products	.7	.7	.6
Textile mill products	1.0	.8	.8
Paper and allied products	.7	.7	.7
Petroleum and coal products	.2	.2	.2
Rubber and plastics products	.6	.7	.7
	$7.0	$6.9	$6.8
Percentage of total employment	10%	7%	7%
Percentage of manufacturing employment	37%	34%	34%
B. *High Technology*			
Machinery except electrical	$1.9	$2.5	$2.5
Electrical and electronic equipment	1.8	2.1	2.1
Transportation equipment	.6	.8	.8
Instruments and related products	.5	.7	.7
• Chemicals and allied products	1.0	1.1	1.1
	$5.8	$7.2	$7.2
Percentage of total employment	8%	8%	8%
Percentage of total manufacturing employment	30%	35%	36%
C. *Other Durable and Nondurable Goods Including Food and Kindred Products and Tobacco*	$6.3	$6.2	$6.1
Percentage of total employment	9%	7%	7%
Percentage of manufacturing employment	33%	31%	30%

a. Not seasonally adjusted.
Source: Survey of Current Business.

Table 6-6. Average Hourly Earnings per Worker for Selected Periods.[a]

	1972	1980	1981
Average hourly earnings per worker	$3.67	$6.66	$7.25
Mining	4.41	9.17	10.05
Construction	4.03	9.94	10.80
Manufacturing	3.81	7.27	7.99
Transportation and public utilities	4.64	8.87	9.70
Wholesale and retail trade	3.01	5.48	5.93
Finance, insurance, and real estate	3.42	5.79	6.31
Services	3.23	5.85	6.41

a. Not seasonally adjusted.
Source: Survey of Current Business.

to realistic initiatives. Theory helps to lay out those issues that are more government-oriented initiatives. The best managerial practice helps to determine what the corporate issues are that require policies from the perspective of the firm. It also clarifies what governmental actions might benefit the industry and the nation.

Now to a theoretical perspective. To paraphrase the early work of Arthur F. Burns titled "Production Trends in the United States since 1870"; An industry tends to grow at a declining rate, its rise being eventually followed by a decline. Burns had two caveats for his Economic Industry Growth Pattern Theory.

1. The conception of indefinite growth of industries can neither be supported by analysis or experience.
2. No rational basis or empirical evidence for the notion that industries grow until they approximate some maximum size and then maintain a stationary position for an indefinite period . . . once an industry has ceased to advance . . . it soon embarks on a career of decadence.

Burns emphasized a number of limitations to his theory. Among these were

1. Progressive retardation of growth rates need not be maintained during an industry's "precommercial stage" nor in the later stage of "late decadence."

Table 6-7. Average Hourly Earnings per Worker in the Manufacturing Sector for Selected Periods.[a]

	1972	1980	1981
A. Basic Industries			
Motor vehicles and parts	$4.73	$9.35	$10.39
Primary metals	4.67	9.77	10.81
Fabricated metal products	4.00	7.45	8.20
Stone, clay, and glass products	3.94	7.50	8.27
Textile mill products	2.74	5.07	5.52
Paper and allied products	3.94	7.84	8.60
Petroleum and coal products	4.93	10.10	11.38
Rubber and plastics products	3.60	6.52	7.16
Average	$4.07	$7.95	$ 8.79
Average less textile mill	$42.6	$8.36	$ 9.26
B. High Technology			
Machinery except electrical	$4.28	$8.00	$ 8.81
Electrical and electronic equipment	3.68	6.94	7.62
Transportation equipment	4.73	9.35	10.39
Instruments and related products	3.73	6.80	7.43
Chemicals and allied products	4.21	8.30	9.12
Average	$4.13	$7.88	$ 8.67
C. Other Durable and Nondurable Goods			
Ordnance and accessories	$4.08	$ —	$ —
Lumber and wood products	3.36	6.55	7.00
Furniture and fixtures	3.06	5.49	5.91
Miscellaneous manufacturing	3.11	5.46	5.96
Food and kindred products	3.59	6.85	7.43
Tobacco	3.47	7.74	8.88
Apparel and other textile products	2.62	4.56	4.96
Printing and publishing	4.48	7.53	8.18
Leather and leather products	2.71	4.58	4.99
Average	$3.39	$6.10	$ 6.65

a. Not seasonally adjusted.
Source: Survey of Current Business.

Table 6-8. Average Hourly Earnings per Worker in the Manufacturing Sector for Selected Periods.

	1972	1980	1981
A. Basic industries	$4.07	$7.95	$8.79
Basic industries *less* textile mill products	4.26	8.36	9.26
B. High technology	4.13	7.88	8.67
C. Other durable and nondurable goods	3.39	6.10	6.65

2. Growth rates need not hold for the secular trends of even established industries, though it does hold for their "megatrends," which are movements of longer duration than secular trends.
3. Growth rates will hold before and after a structural change takes place. When as a result of a structural change a progressive industry is invigorated or a senior industry rejuvenated, the rule of retardation may not hold for a period of overlapping the before and after states.

The Burns economic theory of industry growth is of little help for today's dilemma unless a firm's decision is slanted to phase out or rationalize the rapid contraction for the domestic steel industry or to emphasize a structural change. There are no early warning theoretical systems that tell of unexpected rises or declines in demands or shortages of supplies. No national policies or designated agencies exist for such responsibilities. Other nations, such as Japan, have established national policies and regulations to handle contracting the expansion of their industries including financial and income policies. Furthermore, they establish new institutions to deal with future potential breakthroughs, technical or economic, before they have an impact on the industry and the national well-being. No theories effectively explain productivity in terms other than manpower and quantity of output. Most theories are incapable of measuring the current or future state of technology or the need for flexibility to current markets and adaptability to future markets at competitive prices. Nor do we have the ability to assess and audit comprehensibly the efficiency and effectiveness of each firm in terms of product mix, process, or managerial abilities.

Figure 6-1.   Directional Policy Matrix—Product X.

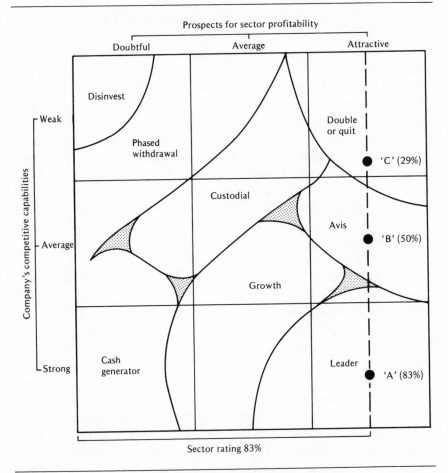

Source: The Directional Policy Matrix, Chemical Planning and Economics, Shell International Chemical Co. Ltd., London, September 1979.

The best management practices can be discussed under a corporate planning and policy matrix. Figure 6-1 shows a policy matrix that measures prospects for sector profitability under three categories: attractive, average, and doubtful. Sector prospects analysis include market growth, quality, feedstock situation, and regulatory aspects. The company's competitive capabilities are rated as weak, average, and strong. The companies' competitive analysis include market position, market capabilities, production capabilities, and product R&D. Ideally, all companies would like to be in the lower right-hand sector, namely attractive prospects for the sector and strong company competitive capabilities—a leader. A good portion of the steel industry unfortunately could fall into the upper left-hand sector. The subsequent management action could be disinvestment or phased withdrawal. A West German or Japanese steel company could well be placed into the "average" sector to implement a growth or custodial policy.

A disinvestment or phased withdrawal is not an acceptable policy from a national point of view, as explained earlier in reviewing manufacturing shipments and employment by basic and high-technology industries. With today's financial market conditions, neither is it an acceptable corporate policy to have national incentives that place the corporations in a custodial average policy situation. Too many other more secure and competitively priced higher yielding capital investments can compete with the steel industry and still maintain the required liquidity. The preferred positions would be Cash generator or Leader or Avis or Double or quit.

When most basic industries in the United States face the unpleasant choices of disinvestment or phased withdrawal, there is a need for more than renewal. National and corporate policies that transform structural changes to our basic industries are badly needed. It is time to develop and target a set of critical issues and to begin to assess their impacts on all sectors of society through creative and innovative management, particularly for the steel and basic industries.

This overview concludes with critical issues facing the U.S. steel industry. Resolving these issues will lead to the eventual formulation of national initiatives required for a stronger, more viable and stable growth of this crucial industry. Moreover, the fundamental questions now confronting the steel industry closely resemble those that will have to be addressed by all U.S. basic industries respectively:

1. Can the steel industry survive foreign competition under free trade policies and still provide for national security, economic well-being and technological leadership?

2. If domestic steel market growth is limited, is it feasible to continue current antitrust regulations? Should there be more concentration in the U.S. steel industry in order to maintain regional competitiveness and meet international competition?

3. In the face of overcapacity and long-life investments in capital intensive facilities, is it efficient to continue competition focused on prices established on marginal prices by individual firms?

4. Is it feasible to continue current tax and accounting policies that do not allow for modern replacement when fierce international competition, age, technological change, or size inadequacy necessitate the relocation or expansion of a plant?

5. To what extent is it necessary and desirable to establish joint venture R&D efforts between government (national/state), higher education, and private industries for U.S. basic industries starting with emphasis on the steel industry?

6. What incentives or national policies are required to accelerate licensing of foreign technology for the steel industry?

7. To what extent is it feasible under a comprehensive security national policy to encourage foreign operations to develop within U.S. domestic markets? What if the operations involve unique and high technology that is necessary for national security?

8. Are tax incentives, including accelerated depreciation, special investment tax credits, and loan guarantees adequate to encourage more private capital formation in the steel and other basic industries? Would orderly long-term public commitment to rebuilding and renovating the roads, bridges, railroads, dams, and water supplies be a better incentive for private capital formation?

9. How is productivity to be measured so as to evaluate continuous capital injection for technology advances, pollution control, quality control and working condition improvements?

10. How far in terms of vertical integration and maximizing advance technology is it necessary to go to develop a stable but strong domestic steel industry?

11. How will the steel industry retain, attract, and develop the necessary creative and innovative managers in view of the current transformation transpiring?

12. To what extent is it necessary to provide sectoral analysis within the federal government to evaluate the impacts of a variety of agencies having an interest in some aspect of a given major pol-

icy decision? This would include monitoring the basic data collection, data analysis, and microeconomic policy analysis for our basic industries, including the steel industry.

NOTE TO CHAPTER 6

1. "Steel's Nightmare—Imports and Layoffs Up, Markets and Spending Plans on the Scrap Heap," *Iron Age*, May 20, 1982.

7 ENSURING U.S. PREEMINENCE IN THE SUPERCOMPUTER INDUSTRY

The computer has been viewed as one of the most basic tools of the last third of the twentieth century. Computer usage for defense, for space exploration, in industry, in education, in manufacturing, and in everyday life underpins the economic opportunities of this age of information and knowledge. Through the 1970s, there were three basic segments that comprised the computer industry:

1. R&D and production of electronic components
2. R&D and production of hardware—computer mainframe and peripheral equipments
3. Development and production of operational software.[1]

Table 7-1 shows the historical lead time between the first working models and first commercialization by nation in the digital computer industry. Their technological status as of 1983 and market position are also indicated in Table 7-1. This table does not take into account the military markets for digital computers. Status as to technology is indicated as dominant, major, and minor. Market position is indicated as worldwide, domestic, or none.

Table 7-1 reflects two types of government policy toward the indigenous computer industry. One policy encourages the use of computers without R&D and production capability. The other promotes the development of a full-scale computer industry focused on both domestic and international markets.

93

Table 7-1. Historical Lead-Times and Current Status in the Computer Industry, by Selected Nations.

Nation	First Working Model	First Commercialization	Current Technological Status	Market Position
United States	1946	1951–52	Dominant	Worldwide
Canada	1955	1964	Minor	Domestic
United Kingdom	1949	1953	Minor	Domestic
West Germany	1941	1954	Minor	Domestic
France	1952	1957	Minor	Domestic
Netherlands	1956	1957	Minor	Domestic
Italy	1957	1960	Minor	Domestic
Sweden	1950	1962	Minor	—
Denmark	1957	1962	Minor	—
Belgium	1960	1963	Minor	—
Austria	1959	—	—	—
Switzerland	1956	—	—	—
Australia	1954	—	Minor	—
USSR	1953	1958	Minor	Eastern bloc
East Germany	1955	1964	Minor	Eastern bloc
Poland	1959	1965	Minor	Eastern bloc
China	1958	1966	Minor	Domestic
Japan	1957	1959	Major	Worldwide

Source: *Computers 1971–1981*, vol. I, Center for Technological and Intradisciplinary Forecasting, Tel Aviv University, August 1971.

Up to the 1970s, it was perceived that the proper use of computers could accelerate the development of a nation's entire economy rather than concentrate only on the R&D and production capabilities to promote one industry, namely, the computer industry. This was particularly the case in Austria, Switzerland, and Australia.

Major European nations such as France, the United Kingdom, West Germany, Italy, Sweden, Denmark, and Belgium, as well as Japan, adopted a policy to foster a computer industry. They believed that they had ample resources for developing an entire scientific and engineering infrastructure as well as electronic components, computer equipment, peripherals, and required software. This policy saw the computer industry as part of a national industrial complex that would become an important force in the nations' economic development.

By the end of the 1970s, only two nations besides the United States had developed significant computer industries: Japan and the United Kingdom. Japan's first commercialization occurred six years after that in the United Kingdom, and seven to eight years after the United States. While Japan was dependent on U.S. imports through the 1970s, it has achieved independence beginning in the 1980s. An outline of Japanese policies for promotion of computerization is shown in Figure 7-1. These policies recognized that the transformation to a computer industry required an investment that was not profitable in the short term, from one to five years. They also acknowledged the need to invest in foreign technologies (i.e., in the United States) to develop an advanced electronic components industry and semiautomated production lines for manufacturing and to promote R&D for architecture of computer systems. In summary, Japan invested in the requirements for a computer industry contrasted to the use of computers for the development of an economic infrastructure. By 1970 there were six Japanese companies in the computer industry.

England, on the other hand, adopted national policies to achieve a rapid increase in computers and computer techniques in industry and commerce plus "a flourishing British computer industry." By the end of the 1970s the United Kingdom was providing 60 percent of their own computer needs for the British government and manufacturing markets for electronic data processing. Their industry consisted of seven computer companies.

The dominant computer industry by the end of the 1970s was in the United States. There were at least a dozen major computer com-

Figure 7-1. Japanese Policies for Promotion of Computerization.

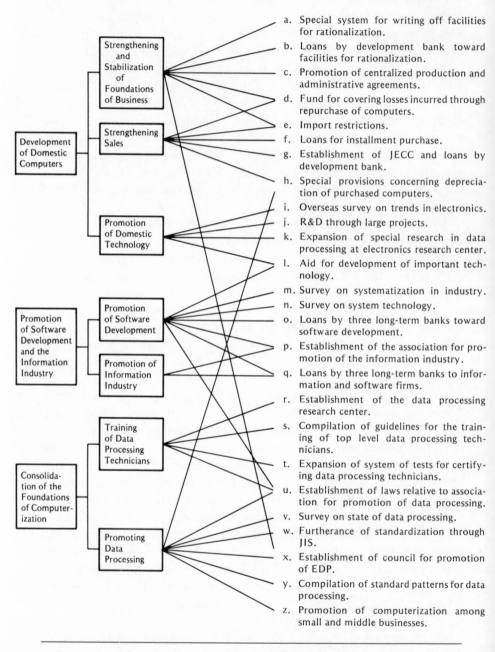

a. Special system for writing off facilities for rationalization.

b. Loans by development bank toward facilities for rationalization.

c. Promotion of centralized production and administrative agreements.

d. Fund for covering losses incurred through repurchase of computers.

e. Import restrictions.

f. Loans for installment purchase.

g. Establishment of JECC and loans by development bank.

h. Special provisions concerning depreciation of purchased computers.

i. Overseas survey on trends in electronics.

j. R&D through large projects.

k. Expansion of special research in data processing at electronics research center.

l. Aid for development of important technology.

m. Survey on systematization in industry.

n. Survey on system technology.

o. Loans by three long-term banks toward software development.

p. Establishment of the association for promotion of the information industry.

q. Loans by three long-term banks to information and software firms.

r. Establishment of the data processing research center.

s. Compilation of guidelines for the training of top level data processing technicians.

t. Expansion of system of tests for certifying data processing technicians.

u. Establishment of laws relative to association for promotion of data processing.

v. Survey on state of data processing.

w. Furtherance of standardization through JIS.

x. Establishment of council for promotion of EDP.

y. Compilation of standard patterns for data processing.

z. Promotion of computerization among small and middle businesses.

Source: Japan Computer Usage Development Institute, Computer White paper, 1970 ed.

panies, hundreds of small and medium computer firms, a half dozen dominant electronic component companies as well as hundreds of small and medium component firms, hundreds of software firms, over a thousand service bureaus, over 75 computer rental and leasing firms, and several thousand by-the-hour computer rental companies. In addition, there were hundreds of universities and colleges teaching circuit designs as well as computer sciences. In other words by 1980 the United States could boast a diverse and entrepreneurial computer industry that did not require large-scale, direct government support. The industry responded to domestic and international market opportunities. It also responded to productivity through lower labor costs by manufacturing overseas, particularly for electronic and other components.

During the 1970s there were a series of seemingly unrelated events that served to alter the U.S. computer industry and thus change its basic character. By 1983 their impacts transformed the worldwide computer/communications markets and created new needs for review of U.S. governmental policies. The series of events was as follows:

1. The U.S. domestic electronic data processing market matured. It became a market for where other nations could sell their products.

2. The first tier large-scale general purpose digital computer manufacturers were shaken out, namely General Electric and RCA. IBM became the dominant research and development manufacturer and marketer.

3. The second tier large-scale manufacturers (Digital Equipment Corporation, Control Data Corporation, Burroughs, National Cash Register, Sperry, and Honeywell) selected and then expanded into specialized segments of the data processing markets.

4. Control Data Corporation (CDC) became the dominant U.S. scientific and engineering computer company in manufacturing and marketing. CDC has since spun off its supercomputer division into a separate entrepreneurially run company named Ada ETA Systems. In the 1970s two new firms emerged (Cray Research and Denelcor) for strictly the scientific supercomputer market.

5. The supercomputer market was created by needs fostered by federal government agencies for nuclear defense and energy research.

6. In 1964 IBM had developed for the first time a large-scale computer system philosophy (for the System 360) which provided for compatibility of software between its own future generations of

computers. Software programs developed for one model could be run on other, more sophisticated, future models without modification. The enormous competitive impact of this compatibility was not generally realized until the late 1970s. Thus IBM may have established data processing industry standards through operationally compatible computer software. This made it possible for other central processing unit (CPU) manufacturers to compete.

7. IBM strategy with System 360 also established a way of standardizing computer hardware, both with peripherals (storage units and input and output devices) and the CPU. This saw the start-up of a number of competitors in both the United States and Japan.

8. The IBM System 360 was the catalyst for a chain of events in the electronic components field. Because of peripheral interface and software standardization, it became possible for competitors to use components different from that of IBM. This changed the technical and economic performance of the computer market. In turn, it transformed the economic competitive structure of the computer industry in the United States and the world.

9. The IBM System 360, from a large-scale computer point of view, extended the competition to machine design, known as computer architecture. In short, it added scientific competition to the computer industry. This permitted and encouraged creativity and innovation in the computer industry worldwide.

10. Capital investments by the user changed dramatically. The billions of dollars invested in software were not obsoleted by changes in future generations of computers.

11. Competition between IBM and other IBM compatible manufacturers resulted in dramatic reductions of costs of large-scale computer systems and increased the through-put performance of IBM's 370 and 308X systems dramatically. More important, it disclosed that the elasticity of demand for large-scale computers was greater than anyone had conceived, in the order of one magnitude. In short, there was a far bigger market in the United States for large-scale computers than originally anticipated or forecasted.

12. Concentration on scientific and engineering computation for government applications, such as nuclear and defense purposes, limited the number of machines to those restricted government and other laboratories involved in security applications.

OPEC-induced oil shortages gave rise to a need for energy modeling and computations. Nuclear, defense, and energy modeling applications created an initial market for the supercomputer. This resulted in the first working models of supercomputers and their first commercialization before the 1980s. By 1983 the market was fundamentally domestic with the beginnings of an international market dominated by three U.S. companies.

13. In the 1970s, a series of federal government needs for very large-scale data and information processing were addressed. Among them were national policy simulations, presidential reporting systems, early warning systems for technology assessment, material and supply shortages, and other large-scale modeling efforts. At the same time national security giant data evaluation problems arose. Cost reduction and increased productivity needs in the Department of Justice, Internal Revenue Service, and Social Security System through computerization were recognized. At first, many of these applications seemed to be more concerned with data processing and storage than with number calculations. But by 1983 it became evident that both data processing for decisionmaking, data storage, and mathematical manipulation were intimately intertwined. This gave rise to the need for supercomputers along the lines of the Japanese fifth generation as well as the scientific-engineering supercomputer.

14. A number of major universities in the 1970s were involved in advanced physical, natural science, and social science research that required both large-scale data manipulation and scientific calculations for fusion, advanced physics, astronomy, biology, chemistry, genetics, biotechnology, mathematics, statistics, artificial intelligence, atmospheric physics, and meteorology, water system engineering, various engineering and business large-scale modeling, methodologies for macroengineering project management, and more.

THE PRESENT

The global computer industry in 1983 is still dominated by the United States. IBM can be given much of the credit for maintaining American global computer industry preeminence. Because of the range of events that took place in the 1970s, however, two nations entered the decade of the 1980s as preeminent worldwide in the computer industry—the United States and Japan.

The computer industry worldwide market is no longer as simple as it once was. Today it is a complex competitive environment in which both the United States and Japan exert major influence across all segments of the computer industry, which includes the communications industry. Indeed, the marketplace is being transformed by the fusion of two technologies—computers and communications. These two technologies are rapidly coming together. This convergence is changing the nature and competitive structure of each industry. The emerging computer-communications industry will include technologies for applications in areas such as local and long-distance networking, time-sharing, satellites, and laser and fiberoptic transmission.

An examination of current developments in each of these industries is important. The market for the computer industry is expanding day by day. It includes mainframes, the microprocessor, the home personal computer, the professional computer, and a wide range of application software. The communications market is also changing in fundamental ways. Among the changes are the break-up of AT&T into local and long-range networks, the development of satellites, digital switching, cable and mobile systems and the rise of telecommunications. This emerging two-technology industry can be seen as giving birth to competitive markets that were not previously available, namely

- The automated office
- Distributed networks
- Automated data bases and information acquisition services
- Basic and applied research services
- Graphics for industry and commerce
- Software for the leisure and the media industries

The application software systems as well as data bases, information bases, and knowledge bases that service these markets are also expanding.

Figure 7-2 illustrates the convergence of computer and communications technologies and the resulting fused technologies for the future. It emphasizes the fusing of the two lines of developments and shows the interrelatedness of the two industries.

To understand the economic consequences of losing preeminence in the supercomputer industry, it is important to examine key segments of the emerging computer-communications industry. Presently, three U.S. companies are selling the present version of the super-

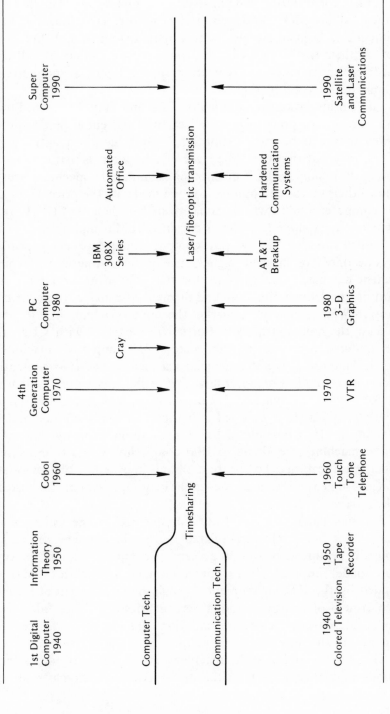

Figure 7-2. Examples of Convergence between Computer and Communication Technologies, 1940–1990.

Source: The Conference Board, "Information Technology," 1972, p. 192, and the IC² Institute, The University of Texas at Austin.

computer for scientific and engineering computation—Control Data's ETA Systems, Cray Research, and Denelcor. Two Japanese firms, Hitachi and Fujitsu, are also in this market. Fujitsu and Hitachi will deliver their first systems in the fourth quarter of 1983. All these American companies are delivering supercomputers and currently dominate the world market.

The world market today is led by CDC and Cray Research. Fujitsu and Hitachi are preparing to deliver their current supercomputers, which they call "vector computers," in production quantities. One of the major attributes of their vector computers is that they can be made IBM-compatible. Current IBM-compatible machines can be tied to their vector computers. It is assumed that the price of the vector computer system will be equal to or less than the CDC, Cray, or Denelcor units, none of which is currently IBM compatible.

Fujitsu's vector through-put computational capacity appears to be one-third to one-half higher than present American machines. Fujitsu has made arrangements for ICL, the major computer company in the United Kingdom and Siemens, the major computer company in West Germany, to market the vector machines in Europe for at least the non-IBM market. Current negotiations with a U.S. firm are underway to market the vector IBM-compatible machine in North America. It is not clear who will market the IBM-compatible vector machines in Europe or how they will be marketed. Fujitsu will market vector machines in Japan, Australia, Asia, and Central and South America. It is believed that these machines will not be IBM-compatible. It is possible to benchmark applications on the Fujitsu vector machine to evaluate its IBM compatibility and to measure its other specifications. To the best of my knowledge, one successful, nongovernment American benchmarking application has already taken place.

Fujitsu's market in the United States will of necessity be earmarked for nongovernment-related needs. Government stipulations generally require that over 50 percent of computer systems be American made. Because most supercomputers in America today are funded by the U.S. government through the Department of Defense, Department of Energy, National Aeronautics and Space Administration, and National Science Foundation, this market is the exclusive province of the three American firms.

The Fujitsu and Hitachi machines are reputed to have a larger computational capacity than current American counterparts. Most, if not all, Japanese and American companies have research underway to develop a giant 10,000 megaflop or more machine by the late 1980s.

Denelcor and CDC are developing major parallel processor supercomputer research projects. Some universities are also researching a 50+ parallel processor supercomputer. The competition is currently in the scientific area.

The marketing competition is for selected segments of the industry. As long as the supercomputer is sponsored primarily by the U.S. government, it will remain American. If it becomes nongovernment funded, the probability is that it will become largely Japanese. The critical dimension will be the source and availability of capital investments. The main issue that our scientific and advanced engineering communities face is how to secure the largest supercomputers for the least cost.

SCIENTIFIC COMPETITION

The previous section indicated that three U.S. firms and two Japanese firms are battling for the supercomputer markets in the 1980s and 1990s. This simply means that these five firms can deliver supercomputers to order today.

On the other hand there are in both these nations significant research projects to develop new supercomputer technologies and equipments. It has been referred to in various media as "The Battle of the Supercomputers," "Japan's All-out Challenge to the U.S.," "The Race to Build a Supercomputer," "Japan's MITI Strike," "Japan Builds a Pillar of the Fifth Generation," "Japan—Here Comes Computer, Inc."

The scientific competition is not only between the United States and Japan. It is also a U.S. intrafirm competition. There are also competitive responses by the United Kingdom and the European community.

The worldwide scientific competition for supercomputers is presently underway. It is quite different from the earlier period during the 1950s and 1960s especially as to sources of funds, means by which research is administered, and the manner of diffusing the innovations within the nation for participation in international markets. An overview by nation follows.

United States

Currently, supercomputers are funded by individual government agencies by ordering a supercomputer from one of the three U.S. firms. Each firm conducts its own directed research and development. Such efforts are generally funded through sales of company products. Their primary sources of funds are R&D expenditures that are tax deductible. New companies have a difficult time raising the necessary capital in the traditional financial markets because of the risk over five to seven years of investing over $100 million to develop a first model. In addition, they do not have the necessary sales revenue and earnings for deduction of the R&D expenditures. Therefore, the probability is very low that as many new firms will emerge in the supercomputer arena as did in the 1950s and 1960s in the U.S. computer industry. U.S. efforts in the scientific competition for the supercomputer industry are summarized in the following paragraphs.

Supercomputer R&D.   Three U.S. firms, CDC's ETA Systems, Cray Research, and Denelcor, have invested nearly 15 percent of their annual net revenues in supercomputer R&D for succeeding generations of computers.

A Joint Venture in Research – MCC.   Over twelve computer firms have agreed to a technological joint venture with a nonprofit research oriented corporation formed in 1982: the Microelectronics and Computer Technology Corporation (MCC). Located in Austin, Texas, MCC has a working relationship with both flagship universities in Texas – The University of Texas at Austin and Texas A & M University.

MCC is financed by the computer firms in the consortium through possible contributions for a 10-year period. Funds are pledged on a three-year cycle. Other firms are being encouraged to participate in the consortium. The participants will be permitted to use patents and other advances developed from in-house research and development. They will have a three-year lead time before such patents are made available to nonparticipating companies. Each participant can utilize the advances as it sees fit for its own product and service lines.

MCC's four research areas are

1. Computer-aided design and computer-aided manufacturing (CAD–CAM)

2. Software productivity
3. Advanced computer architecture
4. Chip packaging

These areas are applicable to the supercomputer as well as other computer/communication technology products and services.

It is expected that over the next 10 years more than $1 billion could be invested in MCC research and development. A current issue and concern for MCC involves antitrust matters. This issue may involve possible civil rather than Justice Department anticompetition suits based on the company's in-house research and proprietary control of the patents.

Semiconductor Research Corporation (SRC). Another innovative type of R&D consortium is SRC in Research Triangle Park, North Carolina. Established in 1982 by the Semiconductor Industry Association as a subsidiary, SRC receives its funding from semiconductor firms, users of semiconductors, and computer system firms. SRC in turn establishes centers of excellence at selected universities and gives contracts rather than grants to universities on a project basis. Currently, they plan to establish at least eight university centers of excellence each funded at a minimum of $1 million per year. In addition, they have placed over 42 contracts with various universities at an average of $100 thousand per year. It is expected that over $100 million will be provided for research and development over the next decade.

The R&D thrusts of SRC are

1. Semiconductor automation
2. Semiconductor materials
3. System and component interaction
4. Reliability
5. Quality assurance and tests
6. Small device structures
7. Research into new methods of device fabricators
8. Research into manufacturing processes
9. Research into packaging and off chip interconnections.

SRC does not plan on proprietary control of patents and will not perform component R&D in-house. Patents and know-how will be made available through the various universities participating in the centers and projects. Through such efforts, SRC R&D can enhance both computer and communication technologies.

Both MCC and SRC have targeted the critical areas for advancing the state of the art for all computers including the supercomputer. Their programs clearly delineate what U.S. computer and components industries believe to be the key bottlenecks facing most firms. Some companies are involved with both MCC and SRC. They are a distinct minority. Many of those not participating seem to be awaiting the resolution of the antitrust issues and other legal concerns.

Defense Advanced Research Projects Agency (DARPA). In March 1983 DARPA announced a new program that started as the "Nth Generation" but is currently known as Strategic Computing and Survivability (SCS) to develop a new generation of superintelligent computers for military use. The SCS program objectives are to develop a system that will allow it to see, reason, plan, and supervise military systems in combat. DARPA's thrust will contain

1. Extension of artificial intelligence research
2. Multiprocessor architecture
3. Innovations in very large scale integrated (VLSI) circuits, including

    a. Gallium arsenide chips, which afford high speed, low power, plus a high degree of radiation hardness
    b. Pilot fabrication of gallium arsenide
    c. High-performance, high-density bulk memory for field application
    d. New packaging including circuit technologies and interconnections (with electrooptics)
    e. High-performance bus structure and access to very-high-density storage.

4. Rapid turnaround and fabrication of integrated circuits

The SCS program will consist of joint projects being carried out between universities and industry at their respective locations as well as within the research laboratories of DOD. Close to $1 billion is being budgeted for this program over the next seven years.

The SCS program has targeted the following military applications.

1. Autonomous systems for advanced vehicles or satellite-control stations

2. Collaborative systems to aid humans in controlling other machines
3. Military assessment systems for war games, battlefield simulation, strategic and tactical alternative generation and solution, and combat operational data, command systems
4. Expert advisory assistance for nuclear planning and logistics, flight operations, and equipment maintenance

The commercialization spin-offs of SCS will be developed under current regulations and governmental procedures.

Stanford University Center for Integrated Systems (SUCIS).   SUCIS is the result of joint research sponsorship by the government, corporations, and the University. The funding for the Center comes primarily from federal government grants (DOD, NIH, NSF, NASA, and DOE). Annual contributions also come from 19 corporations which are involved in the development and sale of computers and semiconductor components. They have already contributed $14.3 million for the design and construction of the Center, as well as for the research and design, fabrication, testing, and applications of VLSI systems. The research and educational program consists of about 60 faculty members, approximately 150 research staff members and 300 Ph.D. candidates. Currently over $30 million is being spent annually.

Among the research tasks at Stanford are

1. Knowledge-based VLSI design
2. VLSI information systems
3. VLSI computer systems
4. Medical and rehabilitation electronic sensors, circuits, and systems
5. Computer-aided, fast-turnaround lab
6. Integrated circuit process models
7. Compound semiconductor and silica-on-insulator research
8. Fundamental studies of semiconductor surfaces and interfaces

Currently Stanford's SUCIS is concerned with the issues of academic freedom, patent rights, copyright privileges, royalty allocations and teaching resource dilution.

Microelectronic Center of North Carolina (MCNC).   MCNC was created as a nonprofit corporation in July 1980. It is funded primarily by the state of North Carolina, which has agreed to provide approximately $43 million out of $50 million for 1981–1985. Participating academic institutions are Duke, University of North Carolina at Chapel Hill, University of North Carolina at Charlotte, North Carolina State University, North Carolina A & T University and the Research Triangle Institute. Three corporations are currently affiliated with MCNC.

The objectives of MCNC are

1. Vertical integration of general and special-purpose machines needed for the next generation
2. Translation of global basic research results into useful technology for industry and government

The key projects include VLSI systems (Vivid); a fast prototyping facility for hybrid techniques; and advanced silicon-wafer fabrication. In addition, there are four projects that use vertical integrated capabilities. These are pixel planes, a Boolean vector machine, a functional program language machine, and image-processing computers. Resultant royalties are divided and administered under each participating institution's policy.

Japan

The Japanese approach to supercomputers has taken a different strategy than that in the United States. Their strategy is to identify and target markets. They have targeted for the 1990s two markets, one for scientific and engineering computation and a second for more intelligent processing of knowledge. The first is referred to as the Supercomputer Program, the second as the 5th Generation Computer Program.

Each program has the consent and support of the Japanese government. Two program teams consisting of university, firm, and government researchers have been formed. Each is funded jointly by the government and six major firms in the computer industry (Fujitsu, Hitachi, NEC, Toshiba, Nippon Electric, and NTT).

In broad terms, each of the supercomputer projects will be jointly funded for a 10-year period at $450–500 million. Once a program is completed, the scientists and engineers will return to their respective institutions. In other words they have built in what can be called a "sunset" provision for the programs, which incorporates an automatic diffusion process for innovation developed during the term of the programs. This is quite a contrast to the diffusion process of the U.S. cooperative technology venturing of MCC and SRC.

The technologies being developed under the 5th Generation Program are in comparative infancy in relation to the program specifications. These "seed technologies" have been identified as follows:

1. Very large scale integration
2. High-speed devices
3. Communications
4. Parallel processing
5. Software
6. Artificial intelligence and pattern recognition

It is interesting to note that, even if the Japanese do not meet these designed specifications for the 5th Generation Computer System, they still expect to find many applications for other markets both before and after 1990. By advancing the boundaries of the technology's state of the art, the Japanese hope to finance a portion of the 5th Generation Program by commercializing earlier technological advances. While the exact nature of the by-products of the 5th Generation Program are difficult to predict, they will permit the Japanese to have an important presence in the following markets: artificial intelligence; computer-aided engineering; decision support systems; and intelligent robots.

The Japanese Supercomputer Program has two important scientifically competitive thrusts: a lightning-fast supercomputer using Josephson junctions or high electron mobile transistors; and an optical computer using optical fibers. Most Japanese government funding for the supercomputer for scientific and engineering computation will take the form of 100 percent grants to industry. Work on these computers started in 1981. The government has loaned 30 researchers plus two engineers from each of nine Japanese firms to work in a laboratory loaned by Fujitsu. Their task is to develop the all gallium arsenide devices needed for computing with light pulses in contrast to electronic signals. A major objective of this program is to develop the new components, including semiconductors, fiber optics, and lasers. These components will in turn have commercial spin-off applications in computers and communications. They have targeted a supercomputer to be developed by 1990 with specifications a thousand times faster than the 1982 U.S. competitive computers. They expect that this will involve large-scale, great speed parallel basic processing involving anywhere between 100 and 1,000 processors working simultaneously.

In addition, they expect to develop their own internationally competitive parallel processing software and hardware. This supercomputer program was started to meet the challenge of IBM's announcement in 1981 that it is planning to develop around 1985 a computer incorporating Josephson junction logic elements, a test approach to the microchip.

The United Kingdom

For the first time in their history, the British have embarked on a collaborative research program among industry, government, and academia that will achieve advances in four key sectors:

1. Software engineering
2. Very large scale integration
3. · Man-machine interfaces
4. Intelligent knowledge-based systems

This approach is a departure from past United Kingdom strategies. It is broadly modeled on the Japanese counterpart.

The cost of the program will be spread over five years and entail investments of $550 million with $316 million from government. Government funds will fund match 50 percent of all industrial funds. The work in the universities will be funded 100 percent by the government. A five-person directorate will supervise the program. The Secretary of the Science and Research Engineering will head the group while four industrial specialists (one from each of the key areas) will also serve on the directorate. The five-person directorate will report to a part-time board.

Europe

The European Commission is trying to establish a five-year European Strategic Program for Research and Information Technologies (ESPRIT). They are seeking funding from the participating countries by November 1983. The Esprit program plans to cover

1. Microelectronics
2. Software technology
3. Advanced information processing
4. Computer integrated manufacturing
5. Office automation

European Consortium. In the interim, three of the largest West European computer companies have formed a private joint research institute located in Bavaria. Compagnie Machine Bull (France), ICL plc (Britain) and Siemens AG (West Germany) will equally finance and run the Institute, which will focus on knowledge processing.

Summary

The scientific supercomputer competition has become a worldwide regional competition for the emerging global market. The current four active groups of competitors are U.S. firms, Japanese firms, the United Kingdom program, and the private transnational European research institute. Two of the scientific competitors do not have major government funding—the U.S. companies and the European transnational institute. Defense R&D and very high speed integrated circuits (VHSIC) programs support the research of two competitors— the United States and the United Kingdom.

Japan has extensive government support both in terms of funds and research scientists for advanced component research. Spin-offs or by-products are being planned by two of the competitors—Japan and private U.S. firms. While Japan tends to target markets, U.S. firms tend to target incremental technological breakthroughs. Only Japan has firm and dedicated funding for 10 years. The U.S. firms funding is dependent upon the market and the individual firm's ability to generate earnings (see Figure 7–3 and Table 7–2).

THE FUTURE OF THE SUPERCOMPUTER INDUSTRY

If the supercomputer industry follows the same policies for preeminence as the computer industry did in the 1960s and 1970s—that is, if it builds a flourishing supercomputer industry rather than focuses only on the use of the supercomputer and its technologies—

Figure 7-3.   Research Funds for Supercomputers, Projections by Nation, 1984–1993.

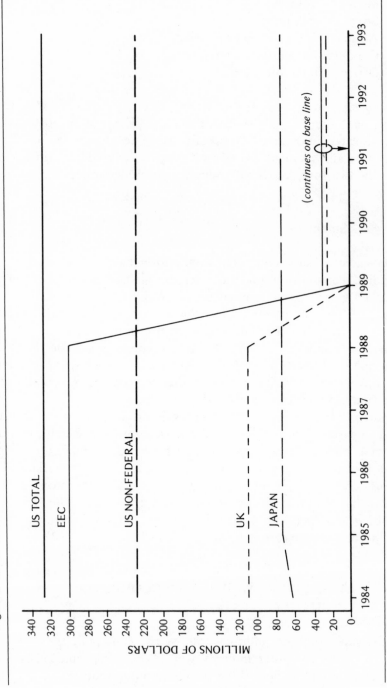

Source: Spectrum, November 1983, and the IC² Institute, November 1983.

Table 7-2. Funding Distribution, U.S. Supercomputer Research and Development, 1984–1993.

Research Institution	10-Year Expenditure (Millions of 1983 $)
Corporate Supercomputer R&D	$ 800
Microelectronics and Computer Technology Corporation (MCC)	1,000
Semiconductor Research Corporation (SRC)	100
Stanford University Center for Integrated Systems (SUCIS)	300
Microelectronics Center of North Carolina (MCNC)	100
Subtotal—private research	$2,300
Defense Advanced Research Projects Agency (DARPA)	1,000
Grand total—U.S. supercomputer research	$3,300

then it is possible to *forecast* such results. Forecasting is an integral part of the innovation process; it is action and policy oriented. Its major assumption is that one can direct a path into the future that can be either self-fulfilling or self-defeating. Therefore, it is necessary to forecast supercomputer annual unit sales, their prices—high, medium, and low—and the projected annual world supercomputer sales.

Annual Unit Supercomputer Sales Estimates

Estimates in the current literature indicate that the market for supercomputers is mixed. There is little or no consensus concerning total sales of supercomputers. Fifty machines have been installed since the start of this year, and some predict a total market saturation point of 100 machines. Others project a maximum of 500 installed machines over the next decade. It is assumed for purposes of this testimony that these numbers are for operations that are not IBM-compatible. When IBM-compatible projections are added, our projections indicate that the market could exceed 5,000 for the next decade. Figure 7–4 shows the annual supercomputer sales estimates.

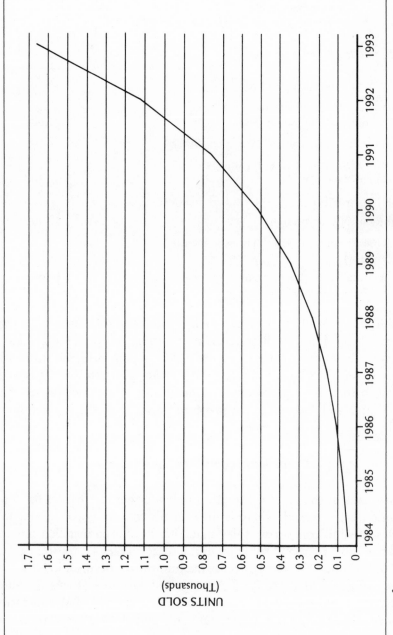

Figure 7-4. Annual Worldwide Supercomputer Sales, Projections for 1984–1993.

Source: IC² Institute, The University of Texas at Austin, November 1983.

Price Projections

In the computer systems industry, learning curve price projections are standard operating procedure. For purposes of estimating world supercomputer sales, Figure 7-5 provides three price projections using 90 percent, 85 percent, and 80 percent learning curves. For the quantities shown in Figure 7-4, the per unit prices are projected in Figure 7-5. For comparative purposes, the years 1984 and 1993 are as follows:

	1984	1993
	(Million $)	
90% learning curve	$10.0	$3.9
85% learning curve	$10.0	$2.3
80% learning curve	$10.0	$1.4

Projected Annual World Supercomputer Sales

Figure 7-6 shows our estimates of annual world supercomputer sales. Predicted on quantities shown in Figure 7-4 and the price schedules in Figure 7-5, our estimates of the total market annual sales of supercomputers are shown in Figure 7-6. For comparative purposes, the total global sales for supercomputers by learning curves are as follows:

	1983	1993
	(Billion $)	
90% learning curve	$.5	$6.4
85% learning curve	$.5	$3.7
80% learning curve	$.5	$2.0

Our projections are significantly higher than others have made for the supercomputer market.

Figure 7-7 shows that a projection of IBM's annual world revenues, exclusive of supercomputers, indicates it will be over $170 billion. We have estimated that the total world computer market will be between $320 billion and $430 billion. Therefore our forecast for supercomputers is less than 2 percent of the 1993 world computer industry market. The IC^2 Institute forecast would have to be quintupled before it equaled 10 percent of the then forecasted world computer market.

Figure 7–5. Learning Curve Price Projections for Supercomputers, for Three Rates.

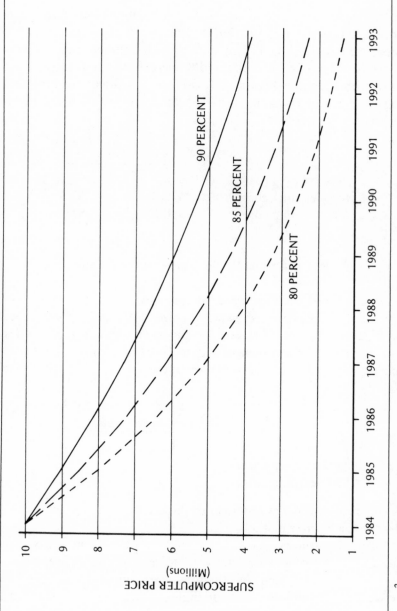

Source: IC² Institute, The University of Texas at Austin, November 1983.

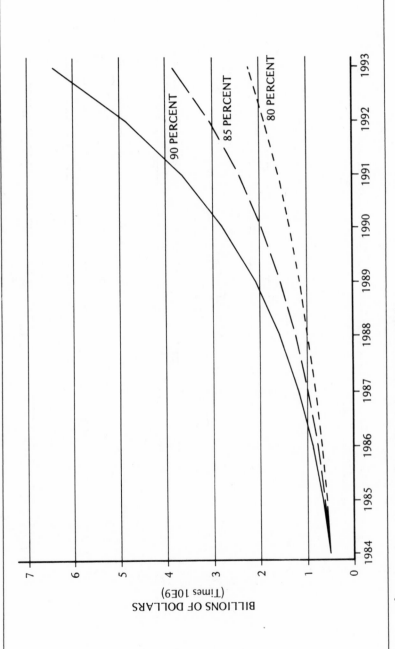

Figure 7-6. Annual Worldwide Supercomputer Sales, Projected Revenue Scenarios, 1984–1993.

Source: IC² Institute, The University of Texas at Austin, November 1983.

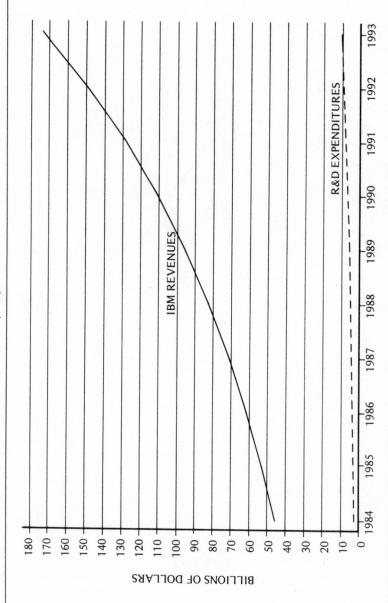

Figure 7-7. IBM Revenue and R&D Expenditures, Projections for the Years 1984–1993.

Source: First Boston, *Insights*, October 4, 1983, and IC^2 Institute, The University of Texas at Austin, November 1983.

On the other hand high sales of $6.4 billion of supercomputers by 1993 could create between 80,000 and 107,000 new jobs. In addition, the industry could require between 100,000 to 250,000 new jobs for operating the supercomputers. These are extremely significant employment forecasts. This employment is about equal to today's total U.S. employment in industries such as furniture and fixtures, and miscellaneous manufacturing; or 1.5 times the employment in petroleum and coal products; or about 1.5 times the employment in leather and leather products. How the United States competitively shares the market is, therefore, very important to consider. Having the biggest, fastest, and most expensive machine may not be enough in assessing economic consequences.

In order to emphasize the economic impact of losing preeminence in the marketplace for supercomputers, it might be helpful to review the recent history of 64K random access memory (RAM) as an example.

The 64K RAM got off to an early start in Japan through a technology venture-sharing, government-sponsored program for research and development of very large scale integration in the 1979 time frame. The Japanese 64K RAM designs were targeted for Nippon Telegraph and Telephone Public Corporation equipment. The Japanese government-sponsored research included three Japanese companies—Fujitsu, NEC, and Hitachi. By 1980 Fujitsu was commercially offering the 64K RAM by the thousand chips per month. By 1981 the Japanese had captured 70 percent of the 64K RAM market. The 64K RAM world market is expected to be over $1.5 billion in 1983 and over $2.0 billion by 1985. It is remarkable how fast a firm can move and take world market share. In the period that the U.S. 64K RAM manufacturers were losing market share, the number of U.S. companies competitively producing 16K RAMs dropped from twelve to only six.

Supercomputer systems are an important factor in developing new chips. Loss of the supercomputer market could well lead to loss of future advanced chips markets for the U.S. One way of looking at the magnitude of such a loss is to examine what impacts the loss of 64K RAM chip market is to U.S. chip manufacturers.

In the analysis shown in Table 7-3, it is assumed that the Japanese chip manufacturers are able to obtain 50 percent of the U.S. chip market by 1993. A more detailed forecast of the U.S. share of the market by source is shown in Table 7-4. The forecast of chips for

Table 7-3. Projections for Chips, 1983 and 1993 (*Billion $*).

	Estimated World Market Demand	U.S. Market Demand	Other Nations' Market Demand
1983	$16	$ 7	$ 9
1993	90	45	45

Table 7-4. U.S. Market Chip Demand, 1983 and 1993 (*Billion $*).

		Source of Supply for Chips		
	U.S. Market Demand	Internal System Manufacturers	U.S. Chip Manufacturers	Japanese Chip Manufacturers
1983	$ 7	$ 2.3	$ 3.5	$ 1.2
1993	45	22.5	11.25	11.25

U.S. demands would increase from $7 billion to $45 billion or by more than 600 percent in the next decade. About one-half of the demand would be provided by system manufacturers' own chip-producing facilities. Over one-quarter would be provided by the Japanese and the U.S. chip manufacturers. The Japanese–U.S. chip market could increase tenfold in the coming decade. Meanwhile the U.S. chip manufacturers would increase their domestic sales opportunity over threefold. The 64K RAM Japanese technical venture has provided a great opportunity for growth for Japanese chip manufacturers. This story of the 64K RAM when coupled to Japanese abilities to design supercomputers that are both IBM compatible and noncompatible provides a very important lesson when considering the future of the U.S. supercomputer industry.

When the total worldwide industry is dominated by IBM, it is important that U.S. supercomputer manufacturers, including IBM, be involved in the development, production, and sales of supercomputers. If Japanese manufacturers capture the whole of the IBM-compatible supercomputer market, they would have over 90 percent of our forecasted market. The remaining 10 percent would also be

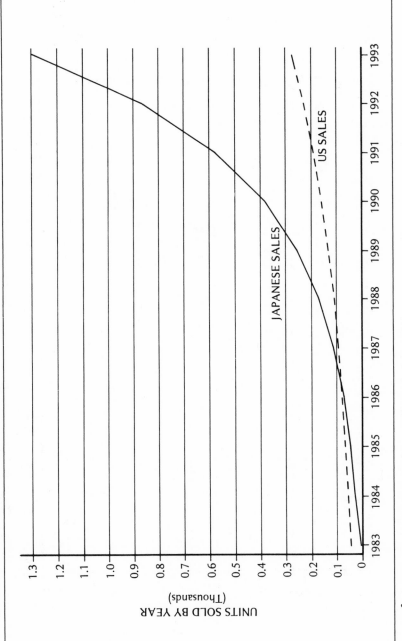

Figure 7-8.   Annual Supercomputer Unit Sales, Projections for 1983–1993.

Source: IC² Institute, The University of Texas at Austin, November 1983.

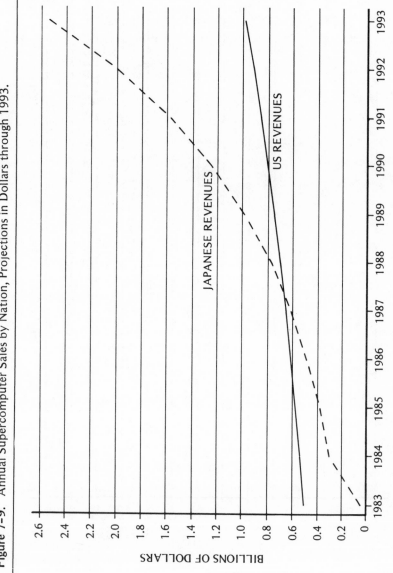

Figure 7-9.   Annual Supercomputer Sales by Nation, Projections in Dollars through 1993.

Source: IC² Institute, The University of Texas at Austin, November 1983.

Table 7-5. Forecast of Annual Computer Sales, 1983–1993.

	Japanese	U.S.
	(Billion $)	
1983	$0.01	$0.5
1993	2.50	1.0

shared by the Japanese as their machines are designed for both the IBM-compatible and noncompatible markets. Furthermore, if they had the bulk of production volumes, they could sell at much lower prices than U.S. manufacturers in the 1984–1993 time frame (see Figure 7-5).

Figure 7-8 forecasts supercomputer unit sales for the 1983–1993 time frame by U.S. and Japanese companies. The forecast assumes that IBM does not enter the supercomputer market until after 1993, nor do the other U.S, suppliers who could provide IBM-compatible supercomputers. However, the U.S. suppliers provide 95 percent of the sales of computers that are not IBM-compatible. The forecasted annual sales for 1983–1993 are shown in Figure 7-9. Sales for 1983 are compared with those projected for 1993 in Table 7-5.

If these assumptions prevailed, the Japanese would clearly dominate the world supercomputer market during the decade. U.S. companies under present plans would not become economically competitive until they introduced their newer models that are currently under scientific competition with the Japanese.

The Japanese firms have already made commitments to the current supercomputer market. This means that they have the ability to meet market demands as shown in Figure 7-4 with relatively small capital investments. In other words Japan was in the same position in 1983 to meet rapidly emerging markets for supercomputers as they were with the 64K RAM in 1980.

ECONOMIC CONSEQUENCES OF LOSING PREEMINENCE IN SUPERCOMPUTERS

The United States is engaged in an international scientific competition in the area of supercomputers. We are also engaged in an international scientific competition in telecommunications. Both of these scientific races are essential for the computer-communications industry for the 1990s and beyond.

The value of scientific exploration and discovery hardly needs to be emphasized. Scientific advances are basic to the continuation of our nation's economic growth. When appropriately commercialized, they can be used to reduce unemployment and underemployment, increase productivity, strengthen our national security, enhance our quality of life, and improve our international balance of trade. But scientific research is more than an economic good.

Scientific preeminence is a reflection of the American culture as well as its enterprise system. Most of us take great pride in the fact that all Nobel Prizes in science for 1983 were awarded to American citizens. Some of us still remember the bitter taste of lost prestige when Sputnik was successfully launched by the USSR in 1957. More important, the products and services from scientific achievements are marvelous attributes of our unique American culture. Other nations have the same desire. Consequently, the scientific race for the supercomputer must be viewed from the perspectives of both national prestige and economic well-being.

The United States can win the supercomputer scientific race, but that does not ensure economic success in a global market. Other nations have become adept at applying American scientific advances to their own needs while improving their manufacturing, financial, marketing, and managerial abilities to compete vigorously in international markets. Japan, the United Kingdom, and perhaps the European community in the 1980s will focus more strongly on R&D and the innovation process in their supercomputer programs. So they may also be as effective in the scientific competition as the United States. As a result, each nation may gain in prestige from its own unique scientific research, organizational R&D structures, and massing of technological and human resources.

In this context the ability to market a product a few months or a few years earlier may be of great value to an individual firm's well-being (and its immediate community). Current economic theory does not emphasize this critical time component. That is, free trade theory maintains that a rational person buys from the cheapest producer even if that means waiting for the product. Individual firms often indicate that such strategy can place us in economic jeopardy—loss of markets at home and abroad. Current economic theory has not advanced to the point where it can cope with rapid diffusion of scientific advances, extremely short technological life-cycles, ever increasing fixed capital investments with shorter economic lives than IRS regulations or tax incentives, comparatively brief generation times for new products, and the rapid appearance and disappearance of markets. In summary, economic theory itself needs to be subjected to intense study to handle these newer classes of problems—more specifically, to measure firms' and nations' efficiency, effectiveness, flexibility, and adaptability in a global market economy when competing with many sophisticated and highly industrialized nations.

In this setting there are a number of economic consequences that can be evaluated. First, the global computer industry during the 1980s can be progressively less dominated by U.S. companies. The 1990s will be even more competitive than the 1970-1980 era. This will not be the result of slipping scientific preeminence. Rather, it is a natural progression to lose share of global markets when other nations become directly competitive. The key question is what share of the future computer-communications market can or should the United States realistically expect to maintain? The global market for computer and communications is estimated to increase from $100–150 billion in 1983 to $500–700 billion (in constant 1982 dollars) in 1993. Currently, the United States scientific and technological preeminence has resulted in our estimation to be at least 75 percent of the current market or $75–120 billion. If U.S. preeminence in its selected fields continues, its share could drop to 50–60 percent. Therefore, its 1993 market would be between $250–420 billion (in constant 1982 dollars). Other competitive nations, including Japan, the United Kingdom, and European common market nations, would increase market share from $25–30 billion to $250–280 billion under these assumptions. Economically, all would prosper even though scientific and technological preeminence was shared. In short, it is difficult to imagine the United States maintaining its current market share over the longer run.

The U.S. supercomputer industry share of worldwide markets could be dramatically below 50 percent by 1987-88 as shown in Figure 7-6. IBM or others must enter the market for the United States to maintain 50 percent or more. IBM could well be ready to announce soon its supercomputer, but there is no overt evidence available on this. The loss of American market share could have a relatively immediate economic consequence in the form of price wars for computers and selected semiconductor chips during the next five years. This could result in less R&D funds for U.S. firms to continue developing the next generation of supercomputers.

Second, the supercomputer scientific competition makes clear that the volume of resources, including human talent, devoted to fundamental science and to technological innovations is limited. In simple supply and demand terms, this means that science and engineering human resources when scarce will be diverted to increasing returns on investments rather than on maintaining scientific preeminence. A useful way to make this point is illustrated by the State of California study which showed that there was a shortage of scientists and engineers to meet their estimated demand for both defense and space markets as well as nondefense markets.[1] The choice in pure economic theory would be to select those demands which provide the highest marginal yield. According to managerial theory, this means selecting those technological products and services which provide the highest gross margin as well as rate of return on investment commensurate with liquidity. Since the results of science do not enter directly into the private economy, the demand for prestige and academic excellence may require public support under such economic conditions.

To maintain scientific preeminence and a significant economic share of the supercomputer market, the U.S. government should consider ways of supporting the domestic market for American supercomputers. One way to support the domestic market while increasing the number of scientists, technicians, and engineers is for the government to assist in placing supercomputers in major universities and nonprofit research institutions across the country.

A more rapid dispersion of supercomputers than the market currently dictates will help to ensure the transfer of technology, which in turn can support widespread continued R&D activities that will expand the whole computer-communications industry. At the same time this dispersion will expand the knowledge and experience available to our human resource base. Supercomputers are still not available in many of our most prestigious academic institutions.

In addition, the supercomputer is needed for other scientific developments in key areas such as defense, space, astronomy, biology, meteorological forecasting, chemistry, genetics, biotechnology, national policy simulation and assessment, and large-scale project management.

Third, the viability of the computer-communications industry depends on not only maintaining but also expanding private sector R&D funding through revenues and earnings. If revenues drop 5-10 percent, major U.S. computer firms will be in jeopardy and may be forced to cut their R&D activities, including work on the supercomputer (see Figure 7-10).

The supercomputer for scientific computation has highlighted the need to recognize that the real issues do not involve catching up with the science or technology or even embracing the Japanese management system or government policies.

The Real Issues

Scientific achievements contribute to a nation's pride and heritage. The most critical economic problem is centered on how to convert advances in science to technology resources—that is, to put them economically into salable products that meet marketplace needs on a global basis. Having the fastest gallium arsenide chip in the development laboratory does not assure tomorrow's supercomputer market. That is the lesson America has learned from the Japanese competition for the 64K RAM chips.

The ability to manufacture at lowest cost as well as meet very tight delivery dates are important economic considerations if preeminence in the marketplace is to be maintained. Advances in chip technology require very large capital investments. There is no end in sight for scientific advances in the density of chips, for the cost of capital, or for the reduction in selling price of the unit (except in theory), as shown in Table 7-6.

Table 7-6. Advances Due to Chip Technology.

Year	Number of Devices on Chip	Selling Price in Production	Estimated Research Capital Investment (Million $)	Refurbishing of Capital (Years)
1960	50	$10.00	$ 5-10	5-10
1970	1,000	1.00	15-20	7
1980	500,000	.01	50-70	2-3
1990	20 million	.001	90-120	1-2

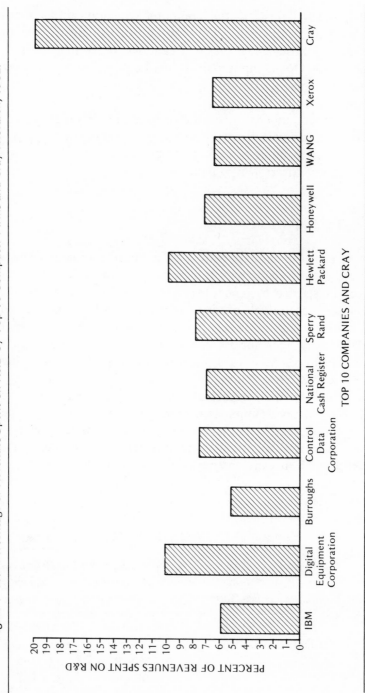

Figure 7-10. Percentage of Revenues Spent on R&D by Top 10 Computer Firms and Cray Research, 1982.

Source: Datamation, June 1983.

The ratio of sales revenues to capital investments is changing dramatically. In the 1970s the ratio was $5.50 of capital investment to every $1 of revenue. In the 1980s it is forecasted to be $2 per $1 of revenue. In the 1990s, the ratio could be a staggering $1 for $1.

We are already beginning to see a reduction of the number of firms in the chip industry. When 16K RAM chips were in production in the United States, there were 12 firms. The 64K RAM chips saw the number reduced to three firms. There are currently four firms in the United States which say they will produce the 256K chips. Concentration in fewer firms may be competitively necessary for the United States to maintain preeminence in the international economy. It is our forecast that Japan will concentrate their supercomputer and large-scale computers in two firms before 1990.

Chips are one of the key economic elements in determining a firm's ability to meet the world competition and in turn maintain U.S. economic preeminence. First, the architecture of the supercomputer is dependent on the chips characteristics. Chips, therefore, provide a competitive edge if they are faster or cheaper or perform more functions or if they combine all three criteria. Second, the ability to make rapid and economical changes in the design stage, the manufacturing process or in the correction of latent defects found at the user's facilities will be of more critical importance in the future under global competition. The costs of changes grows at a compounded rate given geographic distance and progress in the life-cycle of the computer generation.

These distance and progress issues compound the supercomputer firms' capital investment problem. They will have to provide much of their own chip production facilities not only to meet external demands but also to provide for their own internal needs. This is already true of the two major Japanese firms.

There are several economic consequences of such phenomena for national policy consideration. Recent forecasts indicate that major firms in the computer-communications industry will produce about one-half of the total chip market in 1983 or $45 billion for their own uses. They will buy the rest from chip manufacturers—domestic and foreign. Because of the nature of chip production processes, supercomputer manufacturers will be in a position to sell their excess capacity chips that do not meet their internal needs but could be used by others. Price competition, including dumping, could well become as common in chips as in steel today.

We are already seeing that our more creative chip manufacturers are unable to support their future capital needs for both fixed and working capital. Some, like Intel, have already sold a substantial equity position to IBM. Recently, Digital Equipment and Honeywell have made large equity investments in Trilogy Corporation reputedly for the right to the chip and new packaging developments. This could well lead to interesting mergers and acquisitions as well as equity joint ventures. These could have implications for review of current security regulations, tax legislations, and antitrust policies.

From a national technology perspective, the implications are that the current technology venturing arrangements with MCC and SRC may prove adequate for the scientific competition. However, the economic consequences of not being able to produce cheaply enough and deliver in required time may well result in production-oriented technology ventures between medium and smaller sized supercomputer hardware and peripheral manufacturers. It might be necessary to consider the possibility that such technology ventures could include foreign firms. This in turn may necessitate a review of national policy issues of "Buy American," technology export and financing, and extension of high-technology venture capital business.

Continually advancing supercomputer architecture (the design of the computer system) is essential in maintaining economic preeminence. However, the process of designing succeeding generations of the supercomputer system is currently facing critical economic problems.

The period between generations of large-scale computers, just as that between chips, has been substantially reduced. In the 1960s, a generation was 10 years; by the 1970s, the generation was about seven years. Currently, the generation has shrunk to three or four years. Put simply, this means that a firm's R&D personnel must design two new computer systems in the 1980s in the same time that it took to design one in the 1970s. In the words of one chief executive officer, "There is no way that we can do that. It is impossible." What makes this situation worse is the current shortage of skilled personnel. This makes it difficult to keep up with competition domestically and internationally. During the past several years, the salaries and other incentives for key technical talent has risen dramatically. "Frustration" is the only word that describes the current state of our supercomputer manpower situation. The alternative to educating more computer scientists, engineers, and technicians is a longer term solution when the economic consequences are taken into account. For example, now that the Japanese have 70 percent of the U.S. 64K RAM chip market, they expect to maintain at least a 50 percent share of U.S. 256K RAM chip market. Shortage of personnel could well be a serious constraint to increasing or even maintaining the U.S. share of the global computer-communications industry market. It certainly permits foreign competition to target on gaps in our large domestic market and the rest of the world.

National policy must focus on how to continue the United States as a superpower in the computer and communications markets. The supercomputer is the single greatest impact on world communication, automated factories, health care delivery, biotechnology production, renewal of basic industry, and heightened productivity of the service industry, including government. The real task is how to develop appropriately integrated policies, regulations, and support mechanisms that extend the U.S. computer-communications industry. The commercialization of supercomputers for the global market is so tightly structured from scientific exploration to ultimate use, regeneration time is so short, investments so large, and risk so great, that we cannot leave policy considerations to evolve accidently and independently as in the past. One needs only to look at the automobile industry to realize the possible consequences of short-sighted policy development. The computer and communications industry is our future source of large-scale employment; i.e., one out of six. Table 7–7 emphasizes the importance of the supercomputer as a driver for the computer-communications industry.

The consequences of losing economic and scientific preeminence in the supercomputer industry are vast. The supercomputer is a central driver for the rapidly emerging worldwide computer and communications industry. It impacts communication developments, the renewal of basic industries, productivity increases, and the development and expansion of new industries. It is essential in improving our educational structure, fulfilling critical manpower requirements and enhancing our industrial creativity and innovation. It is the seed for encouraging the prolific emergence of technology venture businesses in the context of a private enterprise system that will achieve and maintain U.S. economic and scientific preeminence.

Table 7-7. Effects of Preeminence in Supercomputer Technology
on the Computer/Communications Industry.

Drivers	Area Affected
Industries developed and expanded by supercomputer-related technologies	Robotics/industrial automation
	Computer-aided engineering
	Computer-aided design
	Computer-aided manufacturing
	Computer-aided testing
	Computer-aided quality control
	Biotechnology
	Office automation
	International financial services
	Service industry
	Computer industry
	Semiconductor industry
Revitalization of basic industries	Energy
	Petroleum
	Nuclear
	Steel
	Automobile
	Textile
	Chemicals
Institutions receiving significant productivity boosts	Government
	Defense
	Education
	Research
Communications technology enhancements	Subscribers equipment
	Telephone company equipment
	Overseas carriers
	Satellite carriers

NOTE TO CHAPTER 7

1. State of California, "The Effect of Increased Military Spending in California," Office of Economic Policy, Planning and Research, May 19, 1982.

BIBLIOGRAPHY

"A Big Fight over Tiny Chips." *Time*, August 9, 1982, p. 144.

"A Fifth Generation: Computers That Think." *Business Week*, December 14, 1981, p. 94.

Abegglen, James C., and Akio Etori. "Japanese Technology Today." Advertisement, *Scientific American*, November 1983, p. J4.

Ashley, Steven. "Keeping up with the Japanese: Defense Department to Push for Fifth Generation Computer." *American Metal Market/Metalworking News*, December 6, 1982, p. 7.

Banks, Howard, and Kathleen K. Wagner. "A Matter of Life and Death." *Forbes*, February 28, 1983, p. 35.

Barnes, Clifford. "Who Will Pay for Supercomputer R&D?" *Electronics*, September 8, 1983, p. 87.

Beresford, Roderic. "Opening Salvos Launched in 256-K Battle." *Electronics*, June 30, 1983, p. 107.

Beresford, Roderic, and Robert J. Kozuma. "Ferment and Recovery Stir U.S. Industry to Fight Japan." *Electronics*, June 30, 1983, p. 129.

Bishop, Jerry E. "Can a Supercomputer be Built? Team at IBM Grows More Confident." *The Wall Street Journal*, February 27, 1981.

Blodgett, Albert J. "Microelectronics Packaging." *Scientific American*, July 1983, p. 86.

"Britain Rises to Japan's Computer Challenge." *Science*, May 20, 1983, p. 799.

Bylinsky, Gene. "Japan's Ominous Chip Victory." *Fortune*, December 16, 1981, p. 52.

_____. "The Next Battle in Memory Chips." *Fortune*, May 16, 1983, p. 152.

"Chip Wars: The Japanese Threat." *Business Week*, May 23, 1983, p. 80.

Computers: 1971-1981. Center for Technological and Interdisciplinary Forecasting, Tel Aviv University, Ranat Aviv, Israel, 1971.

"Computers and Their Role in Energy Research—Current Status and Future Needs." Subcommittee on Energy Development and Applications and Subcommittee on Energy Research and Production, U.S. Congress, House of Representatives, Washington, D.C., June 14, 1983.

"Data-Driven Automation: The Education Problem." Carol Truxel, ed. *IEEE Spectrum*, May 1983, p. 93.

Dohler, Gottfried. "Solid-state Superlattices." *Scientific American*, November 1983, p. 144.

Feigenbaum, Edward A., and Pamela McCorduck. *The Fifth Generation: Artificial Intelligence and Japan's Computer Challenge to the World*. Reading, Mass.: Addison-Wesley, 1983.

Ferguson, Charles H. "The Microelectronics Industry In Distress." *Technology Review*, August/September 1983, p. 24.

Gill, Michael D. *Technology Venturing: The Japanese Fifth Generation Computer Program*. Unpublished Professional Report, The University of Texas at Austin, August 1983.

Goldhor, Richard S., and Robert T. Lund. "University to Industry Advanced Technology Transfer: A Case Study." *Research Policy*, June 1983, p. 121.

"Government Plan to Make Fast Computer with Business Is Getting on Track." *The Japan Economic Journal*, July 20, 1982, p. 17.

ICOT Journal, Institute for New Generation Computer Technology, September 1983.

"Industry U.S. and Foreign." *Science*, October 21, 1983, p. 316.

Ingrassia, Lawrence. "Control Data and Cray Start Feuding Again." *The Wall Street Journal*, May 25, 1982, p. 31.

Iversen, Wesley R. "Supercomputers Find New Jobs." *The Economist*, July 28, 1982, p. 75.

"Japan Goes for the Gusto." *Datamation*, August 1981, p. 40.

"Japan Plans New Generation of Computers." *New Scientist*, July 16, 1981, p. 131.

Japanese Economic Journal. Various issues, June 1980–October 1983.

Johnston, Bob. "Japan Builds a Pillar of the Fifth Generation." *New Scientist*, July 21, 1983.

Kolcum, Edward. "U.S. Plans Supercomputer for Defense." *Aviation Week and Space Technology*, April 18, 1983, p. 77.

Lehner, Urban C. "Japan Starting 10-Year Effort to Create Exotic Computer." *The Wall Street Journal*, September 23, 1982, p. 23.

Lester, Richard K. "Is the Nuclear Industry Worth Saving?" *Technology Review*, October 4, 1982, p. 39.

Levine, Ronald D. "Supercomputers." *Scientific American*, January 1982, p. 118.

Lohr, Steve. "Japan's New Test in Chips." *New York Times*, June 5, 1983, p. F1.

Malik, Rex. "Japan's Fifth Generation Computer Project." *Futures*, June 1983, p. 205.

Manuel, Tom. "Advanced Parallel Architectures Get Attention as a Way to Faster Computing." *Electronics*, June 16, 1983, p. 105.

March, Peter. "The Race for the Thinking Machine." *New Scientist*, July 8, 1982, p. 85.

"Microchip Battle: The 64K Battle." *The Economist*, May 15, 1982, p. 94.

Mowery, David C. "Economic Theory and Government Technology Policy." *Policy Sciences*, September 1983, p. 27.

Nakamura, Hideichiro. "Is Japan's Economic Strength Fortuitous?" *Japanese Economic Studies*, Spring 1983, p. 48.

"Now Japan Is in the Running on Chip-making Machines." *The Economist*, January 15, 1983, p. 85.

"Outline of Research and Development Plans for Fifth Generation Computer Systems." Institute for New Generation Computer Technology, April 1983.

Pollack, Andrew. "Japan's Big Lead in Memory Chips." *New York Times*, February 28, 1982, p. F1.

Posa, John G. "What to Expect Next, A Special Report." *Electronics*, May 22, 1980, p. 119.

Preliminary Report on Study and Research on Fifth Generation Computers, 1979-1980. Japan Information Processing Development Center, 1981.

Reich, Robert B. *The Next American Frontier.* New York: New York Times Books, 1983.

Rostow, W. W. *How It All Began: Origins of a Modern Economy.* New York: McGraw-Hill, 1975.

Schefter, Jim. "Fifth Generation Computers." *Popular Science*, April 1983, p. 79.

Selizman, Mark. "The Fifth Generation." *PC World*, October 1983, p. 282.

"Silicon Valley Has a Big Chip about Japan." *The Economist*, March 20, 1982, p. 69.

"Slowly, Slowly on Chips." *The Economist*, March 27, 1982, p. 92.

Smith, Kevin. "U.K. Pursues Fifth Generation Computer." *Electronics*, May 31, 1983, p. 101.

"Straining to Lift Consumption after a Slow Start." *Electronics*, January 13, 1982, p. 121.

Summer, Larry W. "VHSIS: A Status Report." *IEEE Spectrum*, December 1982, p. 34.

"Supercomputing Research and Development, The LLNL Program and Proposals." Unpublished manuscript, Lawrence Livermore National Laboratory, March 23, 1983.

"Technology Update: Information Technology." *Electronics*, October 6, 1983, p. 123.

"Telecommunications: The Global Battle." *Business Week*, October 24, 1983, p. 126.

Texas 2000 Commission. "Scenarios of Performance of the Energy Industry and the Information Technology Industry in Texas." Unpublished manuscript prepared by The University of Texas at Austin Project Team.

_____ . "Methodology Used in Forecasting Performance in the Information Technology and Energy Industries." Unpublished manuscript prepared by The University of Texas at Austin Project Team.

_____ . "Comparison of Historical Performance, Texas 100 Corporations vs. Standard and Poor's 500 Corporations." Unpublished manuscript prepared by The University of Texas at Austin Project Team.

_____ . "Historical Review and Forecasts of Performance in the National Energy Industry 1969-1990." Unpublished manuscript prepared by The University of Texas at Austin Project Team.

_____ . "Historical Review and Forecasts of Performance in the National Informational Technology Industry 1969–1990." Unpublished manuscript prepared by The University of Texas at Austin Project Team.

"The Battle of the Supercomputers: Japan's All-out Challenge to the U.S."
Business Week, October 17, 1983, p. 156.

"The Datamation 100." *Datamation*, May 30, 1983, p. 97.

"The Race to Build a Supercomputer." *Newsweek*, July 4, 1983, p. 58.

Third Quarter Report. Intel Corporation, September 30, 1983.

"Two Nations Race to Build Super-speed Type Computers." *The Japan Economic Journal*, April 6, 1982, p. 9.

Uttal, Bro. "Here Comes Computer Inc.," *Fortune*, October 4, 1982, p. 82.

Verity, John W. "Endowing Computers with Expertise." *Venture*, November
1982, p. 48.

"Who Will Build the Next Supercomputer?" *Science*, January 1981, p. 268.

"Will Japan Leapfrog America on Superfast Computers?" *The Economist.*
March 6, 1983, p. 95.

"Xerox Scientist Joins DOD Supercomputer Program." *Science*, June 24, 1983,
p. 1359.

1982 Annual Report. Cray Research.

1982 10-K Report to the Securities and Exchange Commission. Cray Research.

III TRANSFORMING THE FUTURE

8 PERSPECTIVES ON THE HUMAN POTENTIAL IN TECHNOLOGICAL CHANGE

Any solutions for the problems U.S. business faces will depend upon understanding the consequences of technological change. Our perception of those consequences will affect not only the way in which we link human and technological resources but also the manner in which we approach the decisionmaking process.

The identification of technology as a resource places yet another burden on institutional leaders who are responsible for making complex decisions about the distribution and allocation of resources. Different decisionmaking groups within different organizations perceive and value technology in a variety of ways. Some groups see no need for it. Others see technology as a means of saving society or rescuing a firm's future whenever it is in trouble. However, technology exists and has profound effects. It has the capability of improving or worsening any situation.

Two broad consequences may result because of the importance of current and impending technological developments. The first consequence is to have this control highly centralized. The second consequence is to have this control widely distributed. These consequences are based on the following assumptions:

1. Technology is a body of knowledge.
2. Knowledge is wealth and power.

3. Whoever controls technology controls other resources. Hence, technology is a "master" resource.

It is because of these assumptions that the perceived consequences are centered around the control of technology as a resource.

In the case of highly centralized control, wealth and power could be aggregated in the hands of a small *corps d'elite*. This aggregation could lead to a rigidly bureaucratic organizational structure. Generally, bureaucratic organizations tend to lead to alienation and inflexibility.

The case in which widely distributed control is the consequence of technological development could produce an integrated yet pluralistic society. For individual firms it could broaden the base of participation and decisionmaking at all levels of organization including supervision over robotics and semiautomated functions. Technology gives us the means to distribute knowledge, and therefore power, down to a very local level. With appropriate checks and balances, this same technology could give us the means to reduce the centralization of power and to increase our responsiveness to needs through a more effective structural as well as organizational basis.

The choice between the two consequences and their associated spectrum of alternatives exists. Some technologists have voiced a strong opinion that if trends of the 1960s and 1970s continue, this choice will no longer be available and that a trend toward centralization will be irreversible.

We need to depart from centralization. This departure requires a determined, sustained, and a managerial cross-disciplinary effort. This effort must be well planned and range from small amounts of basic research to a large amount of development, implementation, production, and marketing. To achieve a more pluralistic society as well as increased participation in a firm, initial applications must be carefully selected to integrate technological change with work and organizational needs.

Society has placed the responsibility for solving such problems in the hands of key decisionmakers working through existing institutions. These institutions are characterized by a more or less coherent group of individuals, resources, and values related at least in part to an organizational structure and a formal process of decision and communication.

ALTERNATIVE GENERATION
FOR DECISIONMAKING

I question whether the past loci of organizational decisionmaking can be maintained. We are in the midst of chronic and often unplanned technological change where the value of the new technologies is difficult to assess and the need to adapt to change is vital. To determine the continued viability of the past system of work and organization, we need to ask several specific questions of our decisionmakers:

1. Do they have the time to spare from the current short-run problems and pressures generated by their institutions?
2. Do the operational rules of their institutions permit them to concentrate on anything but the short run?
3. Do they have the motivation necessary to tackle problems whose time frame extends beyond their tenure of office or position?
4. Do they have the current means of distribution of resources (especially technological) to provide sufficient resources to meet the demands?
5. Do the current problem solvers have the appropriate conceptual apparatus to perceive the wider problems facing their firms and all their constituencies?
6. Do they have the techniques, including hardware and software and communication, to structure solution models and procedures?
7. Do they have the information technology required to gather the data for problem formulation, problem solution, and monitoring of results in a timely and effective fashion?
8. Do they have the appropriate organizational structure mechanisms both to solve the problem and to take the necessary implementation steps?

These questions ought to be the boundaries upon which we extend the scientific and methodological borders of knowledge to incorporate technological change for work and organization.

What is required in addition to the answers to these questions is an examination of the premises underlying the responses. We can then ascertain which factors will permit managerial and worker adaptivity.

There will be a critical need in the 1980s for individuals with talents to be

1. Problem formulators—who perceive and formulate the problems facing our various institutions as well as society at large.
2. Modelers—who relate the formulated problems to a unified usable conceptual model that identifies the desired structure of society and institutions
3. Problem solvers or decisionmakers—who translate these problem formulations into understandable opportunities for execution and implementation by the policymakers of institutions
4. Comprehensive auditors—who provide a means for the problem solvers or decisionmakers to validate the acceptability and efficiency of their solutions

Today there is inadequate attention to alternative generation for decisionmaking. Like nuclear reactions, decisions can have unseen yet far-reaching repercussions. If the leaders of our institutions are to manage technological change and not simply be engulfed by it, they need to anticipate the chain reactions their decisions may set in motion.

THE IMPLICATIONS OF TECHNOLOGICAL CHANGES

The potentials of technology for the 1980s have critical implications for all the independent and sovereign nations that are a part of the North Atlantic Treaty Organization or cooperate with it. If we are to advance the quality of life in all our countries, we must understand the implications that technological changes will bring socially, politically, economically and to the individual. In the 1970s most decisionmakers focused technological changes on short-run objectives that were concerned with the bottom line or designed to meet the competition. Longer term capital investments were severely constrained by inflation and capital availability.

The technologies of the next decade will provide for our new growth industries. They will influence changes in opinions, attitudes, concerns, life-styles, and cultural values and affect our defense postures and strategies.

By innovating and then applying technology in anticipation of these developments, we can make the 1980s the age of conscious technological change. Through the judicious application of technology, we can continue to improve our economic, sociopolitical, and cultural conditions. We need not settle for lower quality of life or standard of living. The potential of the emerging technologies for the 1980s makes it possible for us to do more than dream about reaching beyond the status quo.

Without question, technology, tempered with the lessons of the 1960s and 1970s, promises not only stable future growth but also a more productive and fulfilled workforce. All of us who have been a part of technology's science, its management, or support know it is not always predictable, nor does it always achieve precisely what we had hoped. But when treated with respect, concern, common sense, understanding, and general consensus, technology does deliver a fair share of its promises to all mankind.

PERSPECTIVES ON TECHNOLOGY

How do we assess these promises? Only by viewing technology from several "emerging perspectives" can we hope to deal adequately with the dramatic changes in work activities and organizational structures that are bound to come in the next two decades. The technologies for the 1980s must be viewed as a national and a world resource, as a generator of wealth, as the means to increase productivity and international trade, as an area for assessment of public and private risk-taking, and last as an influencing factor for changes in the organization, education, and training of the workforce.

Technology is not simply an "engineering thing," a gadget or even a process. It is a national resource. Unlike natural and human resources, it is not consumed in the process of use. Rather, like a catalyst, it can be a stimulant; or it can be self-generating, as in fusion. The use of technology actually creates more technology. There is, however, no systematic means for allocating or evaluating technology as a resource. Today we cannot tell whether the allocation function is efficient or inefficient or even whether it is working and meeting the objectives for which it was created let alone the needs of society or our individual institutions.

Technology is a type of wealth, one that we do not yet know how to measure for economic purposes. Since we cannot measure technology as an economic resource, our ability to determine its full value is limited. Wealth, of course, is a means of attaining economic, social, and cultural status for individuals as well as a way of achieving institutional objectives and the general welfare of society. It is recognized as perhaps the single most important variable in determining the alternatives of an individual, a corporation, a nation, a state, or a locality. Wealth is the key to power in any political system. Its ownership, control, and transformation determine not only the structure of society but also the success or failure of the system itself. To ensure the continued strength of our economic and political systems in terms of our current institutions, we need to develop ways of estimating the real wealth—that is, the productive wealth—provided by new and improved technologies.

Technological innovation is a prime factor in stimulating our productive capacity and ensuring healthy competitive international trade. We must, therefore, adopt more viable national policies for technological development. Thus far, few if any nations have effectively formulated such critical policies. We can bring about significant short-term as well as long-term gains by encouraging the establishment of an effective working relationship between government, business, and universities regionally, nationally, and internationally in order to strengthen and broaden our R&D environment. Government can be a very important stimulant to technological development. By developing policies that encourage academic and industrial research, strengthen the educational structure, promote a positive business and economic climate, and identify special areas of concern, government can be a positive force in technological growth.

The relationship between the public and private sectors is changing. Each nation's technological needs are linked with other nations' commerce in a number of important ways. In no case is one market wholly insulated from what happens in other countries. This is a fundamental political and economic fact. Shortages can result in a crisis, a comfort, or a boon depending on the circumstances. Some shortages can produce a crisis of national consequences. To reduce the consequences of the crisis puts us in the arena of potential public risk-taking. When such an event threatens national security either economically or militarily, there is a public risk. Investments in some critical technological areas may be so large that the private sector alone is unable to assume the potential risks. Petroleum import dependence, for example, is both a factor of national economic and technological importance as well as a threat to national security. It is appropriate to consider the risk involved as a possible public venture to be implemented as well as supplemented by our private firms.

We need effective technological management training at all levels in both the private and public sectors in operations as well as research. This is in addition to scientific and engineering education and training. Over the next decade a variety of changes in technology are likely to occur that will significantly affect all institutions. Any predictable developments in technology, however, can only come about as a result of the actions of public and private institutions. Thus changes in technology become matters of what we decide rather than merely events to be predicted. Conjecture, of course, will play a part, but the emphasis should be on the transformation of the managerial component. Conjecture is a matter for experts; management is a matter for managers; the former is sterile without the latter. Management of change depends on how we manage the creation and application of technology and its acceptance as well as constructive contributions by the work force. Technology management education and training is central to this function and responsibility.

RENEWED ENTERPRISE SYSTEM

The allocation of human and technological resources takes place within an institutional setting. Technological change is occurring with such velocity that it is difficult, if not impossible, for individuals and institutions to respond. As change in the environment accelerates, more novel first-time problems arise. Traditional institutional forms may prove inadequate, and innovative thinking may be required if we are to keep pace.

In the 1950s and 1960s, the federal government in the United States financed research and development through its focus on military preparedness and need. In the 1970s the government's emphasis shifted. Medical, environmental, and human delivery systems gained prominence as our government directed funds toward federal programs aimed at broadening social welfare. Currently, there is strong support for a return to greater allocation of money for defense R&D

expenses. The linkages of such efforts to more nondefense applications have not yet been addressed but need attention.

Technology from 1950–1970 was generally applied to the advancement and marketing of a particular segment of an industry such as integrated circuits for new generations of large-scale computers. The technologies of the 1980s will not be solely used in this manner. A clustering pattern will be the hallmark of the 1980s and 1990s and will be based on prioritized economic and social needs. It will complicate the organizational structure as well as increase the complexity of training the workforce. In the process, however, it could well lay the groundwork for the developments of a renewed enterprise system. To accomplish this, the private or public sector or both will have to develop a new, integrated incentive program that will include such diverse elements as expanding perquisites, stock options, security systems, pensions, and bonuses in addition to attractive salaries. The allocation of human capital is an institutional process that is profoundly affected by technological change. The objective is to ensure adequate manpower supply in appropriate institutions at the proper time.

Individual and institutional goals are complex and sometimes contradictory. The motivation of specialists, who are always in short supply, is changing. Specialists will tend to be more impatient; they will be in positions to demand immediate gratification. Unlike the others in the workforce, who are willing to take risks and seek to optimize the economic resources of the organization, specialists will be more apt to move out of the organization to pursue their own objectives. Consequently, this independence and increased mobility among skilled specialists may present a real skilled labor shortage in the years ahead.

The personnel requirements for the technologies of the 1980s will create a major societal displacement. Millions of workers who now do only repetitive jobs will need to acquire new skills. Technological change is likely to have three dramatic impacts on the general work force. First, machines will take over repetitive work tasks at an accelerated rate. Second, elementary decisionmaking will become part of the mechanized process. And third, human resources will be freed to supervise more complex machinery and assume a wider decisionmaking role. How should we approach these developments? Required training and upgrading must be related to appropriate incentives.

MEETING INDIVIDUAL AND
ORGANIZATIONAL NEEDS

Conscious technological change presents us with a different kind of challenge: to organize work in such a way that the individual has the appropriate incentive to keep updated. This will require us to fulfill the needs of the individual while meeting the needs of the organization. Organizational leadership will have to facilitate the adaptive process and thereby reduce resistance to change. Responsible management should seek active collaboration and not simply passive acceptance of new ways from the workforce. More active participation will mean increased flexibility in the workplace, the advent of the electronic cottage, and the customization of products and services.

To be successful within our technological society, institutions must attract men and women who accept responsibility, who handle even larger tasks and who adapt swiftly to changed circumstances and the new technologies. This type of workforce will be less pre-programmed and will react faster to changes in the environment. They will tend to be complex, individualistic, and proud of the ways in which they differ from other people. Workers who seek meaning, who question authority, who want to exercise discretion, or who demand that their work be socially responsible may be regarded as troublemakers in some institutions, but the new technological society cannot run without them.

In the past, theorists worried about providing too much leisure time for fear that workers would not know what to do with it. At the same time, society was providing the requisite capital to build the infrastructure for recreation and leisure. Currently, people are demanding more time to use as they wish. They are even willing to buy larger segments of their own time. We need to become more aware of the trade-off between individual time and remuneration and then more effectively balance the two with appropriate incentives.

Comprehensive or full-scope audits of all phases of management's responsibilities and activities will become a reality in the 1980s. These audits will have to deal with long-range plans, manner of governance, the institution's contributions to society's general welfare and management effectiveness. All of these deal with the allocation of human and technical resources. In this context the essence of management in the 1980s must be foresight, calculated action, and accountability.

TECHNOLOGY IN MANAGERIAL EDUCATION

I would like to conclude this chapter with some remarks on my particular area of expertise, that is, the management of a professional school. As dean of a major American business school, I am constantly reassessing what our role as an educational institution ought to be in our complex and rapidly changing technological society.

Effective manpower planning is directly related to education and training. Training focuses on specific jobs and skills and prepares one to cope with change. Education focuses on adequate support systems and research and prepares one to manage change. In both cases experience plays a crucial role and organizational management must find ways to provide the necessary experience. In addition, management should determine on a timely basis what the opinions, attitudes, and concerns of the work force are and then take appropriate action to provide adequate training and education.

Higher education has been exemplary in education of scientists and technologists. It must continue to meet this responsibility. However, I have been asking myself what will the technologies for the 1980s require of professional schools in their task of preparing students for managing technology. Because the education process must be cross-disciplinary, it will be necessary to broaden the scope of management education at the master's level. We will need to include many existing as well as some new academic disciplines including science, computing, business, law, and public affairs. Managerial education must include technology as a necessary function with the same importance as marketing, finance, production, accounting, and human resources.

The job of the professional school is essentially twofold. On one hand it must import problems and develop them into issues suitable for research aimed at solutions. On the other hand it must export and communicate results. This importing and exporting process should be geared around several strategic research areas within the overall context of work, organizations, and technological change:

- Managing productivity, efficiency, and competitiveness
- Managing innovation, research, and development
- Managing international business
- Managing strategic relationships and social responsibilities
- Managing human resources, including manpower, compensation, rewards, and working life
- Entrepreneurship, business development, and capital venturing
- Financial management and markets including capital requirements and investment decisions
- Managing information and management information systems
- Managing the environment in the interests of quality of life
- Developing new growth industries
- Assessing technology as a national and world resource
- Evaluating technology as a value resource
- Analyzing public risk
- Assessing the influence of technology on organization, education, and training.

Responsibilities of Professional Schools

If professional schools are to develop curricula that will meet the needs of our changing technological society, they must integrate three responsibilities.

First, they must emphasize situational and strategic management control. For too long, managers of firms have paid little attention to the scientists and engineers in their organizations, while the scientists and engineers have ignored the issues and needs of managers. What educators need to do is to redesign the educational process in management programs. Professional schools must provide the crucial link between basic sciences and management practice. That link can be provided by a new core of professionals who demonstrate genuine entrepreneurial skills. These highly qualified techno-socio managers will be able to deal effectively with this age of conscious technological change. They will be able to recognize, understand, and implement the fundamentals of both the physical and social sciences and apply them to social needs as well as specific issues on national agendas.

Second, professional schools must focus on comprehensive audits. We need to work to create an appropriate system for evaluation that provides real accountability. In addition to education for the management of technological change, the academic community has a responsibility to do the research required to develop an acceptable body of knowledge in the area of compliance and comprehensive audits.

Third, professional schools must expand our state of scientific knowledge by developing methodologies and techniques to deal with complex problems involving our technological and social evolution. An example of such a problem is the allocation of world resources to meet the needs and secure the rights of all people. Other macro-engineering problems include concerns about pollution, scarcity, social welfare, energy, and public risk. The management of such large systems requires that the leaders of our institutions exhibit the abilities to conceptualize multiple objectives, to interact with other economic, social, and cultural institutions and to operate within a highly dynamic environment. Research in education should, therefore, be directed toward establishing a way in which man and society will reconstruct the world based on the technological change that is taking place.

What I am advocating is an increased scope for professional schools if they are to meet perhaps the most demanding challenge of the next century: namely, to manage our human resources in a technologically based society in such a way that we actually anticipate change and not just accept or react to it. We must develop the ability to organize work in such a way that for most individuals—regardless of race, color, creed, sex or intelligence quotient—work becomes more complementary to human needs and thus more fulfilling and self-satisfying.

9 CREATIVE AND INNOVATIVE MANAGEMENT
A New Academic Frontier

Educating and developing creative and innovative individuals is not a new academic frontier. Educational systems have always had the goal of producing scholars and graduates who will extend the frontiers of knowledge and benefit society. The primary focus of education, especially at the graduate level, has been to create depth within the specific discipline rather than a horizontal approach that integrates academic disciplines for the solution of important societal issues. Academic institutions have concentrated on scholars to extend specific fields of study.

Only a few of our creative and innovative scholars in and out of academia have been willing to forsake their specializations to concentrate on management in the broader sense. Of those who have become creative professional managers, few have returned to academia to educate future teachers, researchers, and management leaders that our complex society requires.

The thesis of this chapter is that the university of tomorrow must prepare itself to research and teach creative and innovative management as a new discipline that requires understanding and implementation of solutions to generalized as well as specific problems of society. The solutions will require knowledge of the fundamentals of both the physical and the social sciences' best practices. Tomorrow's managers of key institutions must understand that resources include science, technology, and information and that these are also assets for the solution of the nation's problems. Managers need to understand that information, science, and technology are not free economic goods but are assets to be used, planned, earned on, and replenished.

Currently, a new type of manager is required to operate under new principles of governance. The distinction between owner or entrepreneur and professional manager has to a large extent disappeared in the past decade. The functions of professional managers have been extended by newer and more complex organizational structures, newer governmental regulations and relations, and changes in generally accepted ethics and morals. In sum, our society has changed dramatically. This change has been characterized by a gap in the management knowledge base. Society has directly affected the management of various institutions, while these institutions have in turn forced society to reexamine basic values and responsibilities.[1] What do these changes in basic values and responsibilities mean for the new frontier for creative and innovative management?

Clark Kerr, former Chancellor of the University of California, made the following observations:

> I think that we shall have increasing demands for communicative links across
> . . . intellectual interstices, as well as demands for the generalist who can view
> problems as a whole and can foresee the new problems that grow out of answers to current questions. We must find a way to restore a sense of unity to
> the intellectual world.[2]

Creative management involves the abilities to take a problem or crisis and develop its issues, generate alternative solutions, and select feasible initiatives from among the alternatives. Furthermore, creative and innovative management includes the ability to use initiatives as a first step to solutions. These initiatives need to be monitored to determine that the actions are indeed solving the problem and not creating new problems.

Issues are problems defined well enough to being the solution process. Thus the creative aspects are turning crises or ill-defined fuzzy and sometimes messy problems into viable issues. Creativity is the input to innovations; innovation is actualization of solutions to problems and crises. Creative and innovative management is concerned with understanding the state of the institution and that of society in order to improve each in terms of the general welfare.

Traditionally, managers have been concerned only with their institutional well-being; their focus has been on the status quo and the shorter run. However, the environment in which all managers operate today is no longer traditional, particularly in the case of managers of our large and dynamic-growth institutions. Therefore, now is the time to begin the process of creating an academic field for creative and innovative management. We need to find examples and role models for students to study and relate to. Fortunately, there are many techniques, methodologies, and tools to offer to the discipline; and numerous managerial problems and crises need to be organized and solved.

There is no need at this time to decide which current academic discipline should be assigned the leadership and coordinating role in this new frontier.

Creative and innovative management will not be confined to business graduates. In fact, it never has been. Creative and innovative management graduates will be cross-disciplinary—in Kerr's term "generalists." As a field of study, creative and innovative management needs a home where the appropriate set of disciplines can form a consortium and work together in the development of a distinct body of knowledge to be taught and used.

The evolution of this new frontier can be examined from three key perspectives that are both personal and professional:

1. The role of The University of Texas at Austin in the evolution of creative and innovative management as an academic discipline
2. First initiatives for the creation of a journal for the identification and extension of creative and innovative management
3. Structuring areas for creative and innovative management research and experimentation

ROLE OF THE UNIVERSITY OF TEXAS AT AUSTIN IN THE EVOLUTION OF A NEW ACADEMIC DISCIPLINE

The University of Texas at Austin provides an interesting example of the academic evolution of creative and innovative management. It has in place some of the required policies and practices for cross-disciplinary education and research as well as a sufficiency of all resources. The more important of these are

1. Universitywide policies for interdisciplinary faculty appointments have been successfully implemented for more than 20 years.
2. Many nationally and internationally recognized academic disciplines and outstanding research and teaching scholars participate. Currently, there are over 78 academic departments and over 300 Professorships and Chairs.
3. Already a large number of joint degree programs are in place among the 14 colleges. These programs integrate a number of academic disciplines important in the solution of societal problems and issues.
4. Facilities for teaching, research, and learning are among the most modern in the United States.
5. The University is not solely dependent on state funds. It receives a large share of the return on the Permanent University Fund and has substantial gift and endowment funds.
6. The University of Texas System, of which The University of Texas at Austin is a part, allows access to additional faculty and disciplines in health science, nursing, and dental and medical care—including research.

As early as 1966, the Regents, the University of Texas System, and The University of Texas at Austin Administration took the lead for business education to be extended into the management of technical and intellectual resources. By September 1966 the College and Graduate School of Business faculties accepted the following challenge:

> To train the managers of the second half of the 20th Century. More specifically, the College must educate future managers of the technical and intellectual resources of our nation. In this respect, our curriculum must be cross-disciplinary as well as embracing new methods and techniques.
>
> It is our firm belief that the managers for the second half of this century must deal with emotional as well as technical changes . . . must learn to converse in the appropriate language of mathematics . . . communicate with and manage scientists, engineers, accountants and artists . . . use new tools for effective planning and control, strategic and tactical decision making . . . understand and implement the social value system of our nation. To the best of our knowledge, no other school of business has set forth such objectives.

It was recognized that the implementation of these objectives would require the establishment of a sound research program; a review of the establishment of our undergraduate, master's and Ph.D. programs in consonance with the objectives; and the establishment of a required executive development program.

The research programs directed toward management initiated in 1966–67 were

- International Resource Management
- Management of Research
- Biomedical Research and Transfers of Technology from Aerospace
- Economic Development, Health Maintenance, and Transference of Technology
- Information Processing
- Cognitive Machine Processors
- Marine Science and Related Business Potentials

The key requirement was the establishment of management curricula with a system and structure for those who would manage our technical and intellectual resources. Educating managers of technical and intellectual resources must be distinguished from creating a discipline for creative and innovative management. The former provides for the effective development of middle managers of the nation's high-technology sector as well as updating the traditional business functions. The latter is more concerned with the creative and innovative management of all resources and their applications in meeting societal and general welfare needs. In its broadest context the focus is on a private enterprise system and its interface with the public sector.

The creative process used at The University of Texas at Austin to develop the curricula for management of technical and intellectual resources is now in place. The current curricula accommodate the notion of system and structure. The notion of system is that graduates will have more than one career. The structure is based first on a core area divided into required knowledge modules; and second, on elective courses that can be taken in any of the 14 colleges and 78 academic departments to support future career choices.

At this point it is appropriate to enumerate briefly some of the problems that led to a need for a review of management curricula in 1966:

1. Development in management in the United States since World War II had closely paralleled the growth of our nation's technology. Advances in the developments of both management and technology are inextricably interwoven.
2. There was increasing recognition for the need of management in fields other than business—in government, biomedical research, health and welfare, urban planning and international trade.
3. Important academic curricula revisions and discussions on interdisciplinary approaches were taking place on most campuses.
4. Many professions had recognized that they must be able to keep pace with the growth of new knowledge. Equally important, there was increasing recognition for continued professional education to reduce the obsolescence rate, or conversely, to maintain the degree of knowledge required for competency.
5. National policies were being established in social areas.
6. Attitudes of management were changing toward the utilization of scientific research as a basis for managerial decisionmaking.

The routine requirements of the past two-thirds of this century are rapidly being replaced by machines and complicated by overseas competition. The U.S. business education system has been geared to educate and develop people for an industrial need that can be generalized as "routinized" or mass production and distribution.

The latter part of the twentieth-century industrial state imposes on our education system the task of the increasing development of people for nonroutine tasks. Problems associated with this can be characterized as follows:

1. The end products are few in number and often one of a kind in contrast to mass-production products.
2. They are large in scope and often require interrelated government, university, and industry efforts to help solve the problems.
3. The problems are characterized as complex and require "integrative systems" for their adequate solution.
4. The problems can be characterized as "messy" and "fuzzy." There is no clear-cut, acceptable solution to them; often current

methods, techniques, and tools must be supplemented with ingenuity and individual creativity and judgment.
5. The problems are one of a kind, and the solution to each is inapplicable to any other problem.

There are two underlying needs to all these nonroutine pursuits. They demand large infusions of technical and intellectual resources, such as individual scientists in both the social and physical sciences, engineers, and other professionals with service personnel and technicians as aids to these professionals. They also require the information necessary for the solution of the nonroutine problems. The key requirement is managers with the ability to identify and formulate problems and to manage the technical, intellectual, and information resources.

Meeting the supply of talent for nonrepetitive tasks will bring changes in the way these resources are managed. There are good reasons for this; intellectual resources are scarce and their supply is relatively inelastic.

In short, the change has set up a self-amplifying system in the demands for intellectual resources. Technology generates new advancements, which, in turn, generate a still greater need for sophisticated intelligence. The task for management education is not merely to select the gifted or excellent student for training but to develop on a broad front the levels of skills—new and existing—to meet the requirements for this change.

Historic development of curricula for management shows that it proceeded very slowly from zero courses to the series of specialized professional and academic fields that we have today. Highlights of these developments are shown in Figure 9-1.

For many years business management was made up of gifted, non-business trained, creative, and innovative individuals.

Our perceptions of the importance of science, inventions, and innovators for creative and innovative management were honed by the seminal work of Professor Walt W. Rostow, in his book, *How It All Began*, who wrote:

Scientists, Inventors, and Innovators. Stemming from the Faustian outlook, the pursuit of principles of maximum generality by the experimental method was understood, from an early stage, to open the way to practical and profitable inventions and innovations.

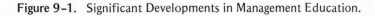

Figure 9-1. Significant Developments in Management Education.

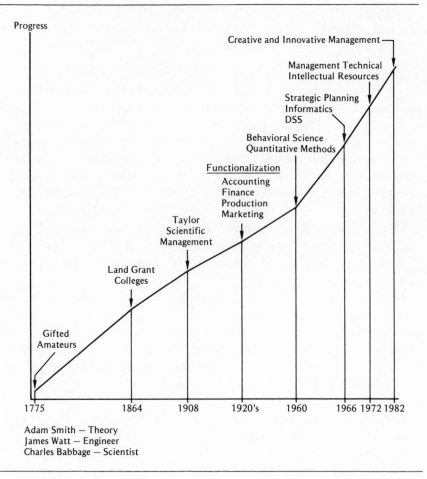

This was, of course, a central theme of Francis Bacon before Newton emerged on the scene, and, from Galileo's interest in shipbuilding, mine pumps and artillery to Newton's fruitless alchemy, some of the scientists interested themselves directly in practical matters. The Baconian linkage of science to material progress was greatly strengthened by the web of osmotic ties that grew up between scientists, inventors and entrepreneurs . . .

The three indirect linkages set out here between the world of science and those of invention and innovation were powerful. They withdrew, as it were, the graphite rods from the atomic pile and permitted an ultimately explosive set of interactions to occur.[3]

Formal business training started in the United States about the time of the land-grant colleges. Its need was first recognized in the agriculture sector. Taylor produced the methodology for scientific management about 1908, and his methodology is still taught in industrial engineering courses. By the 1920s the United States saw the functionalization of business become important in the educational process. The 1950s saw the rise of the behavioral sciences and management sciences and quantitative methods. These were all important steps in the progression of management education and theory.

The explosion of information and the management of technical and intellectual resources required that management curricula take another quantum jump at this time for the development of a new class of managers, management faculties, and university administrators.

Now there is a foundation in place at the Graduate School of Business which has been extended to and coupled with the Lyndon B. Johnson School of Public Affairs, the College of Engineering, the College of Communications, and the School of Law. This environment allows the new discipline of creative and innovative management to be developed. While there is still much to be done, we have already pioneered the directions to open up this new frontier.

A JOURNAL FOR CREATIVE AND INNOVATIVE MANAGEMENT

The time is right for establishing a multidisciplinary journal for eclectic creative and innovative management articles. Creative and innovative management articles are not being published. Very few journals will even accept academic articles in this field for publication. Still fewer professional journals will accept "how to do it" articles even if they could get the creative and innovative managers to write them. Despite this, there are new theories, methods, principles, and selected programs used in creative and innovative ways that should be published in academic journals.

Several initiatives are necessary to extend this new discipline:

1. Identify the large amount of specialized academic work that lends itself to broadening this disciplines
2. Recognize innovative and creative managers and firms

3. Understand social innovations and large-scale programs and projects
4. Commission surveys and syntheses.

A significant number of successful creative and innovative managers have established and developed dynamic organizations and have successfully pioneered and implemented many scientific, technological, and social innovations. Their experiences need to be gathered, analyzed, and evaluated to provide us with a rich history. These analyses go beyond case studies, institutional histories, history of technological innovations, or archival accumulations.

Creative and innovative practitioners often find it difficult to determine whether their contributions are to management or to a specialization. At times they have found that formulation of issues and initiatives is not deemed academic or as important as a specific technique or methodology. Consequently, there needs to be a place where creative and innovative constructs and their usage can be published and deemed important. Constructors, when properly done, can provide creative solutions without being subjected to the normal standards of scientific approach; e.g., cause and effect. The lack of acceptable places to publish diminishes the interest of academicians to invest their time in this pioneering field of current and future needs.

Management scholars in many academic institutions, professional groups, and corporate laboratories are engaged in developing new operations research techniques, new computer algorithms, and new models directed toward solving important problems for the development of the creative and innovative management discipline.

New classes of management planning and control decision problems to be investigated by management scholars and scientists have several characteristics:

1. They involve more than one level of management.
2. They involve highly complex and diversified activities.
3. They deal with service processors.
4. They involve interrelationships between economic, social, and cultural objectives of individuals and institutions.
5. They require the handling of great volumes of data.
6. The time frame for the solution of these classes of problems is compressed.

7. The effects of possible alternative solutions are far-reaching in terms of both timing of impact and number of individuals affected.

Any attempt to address these new classes of problems must go beyond merely developing new techniques, algorithms, and models and searching for new applications for existing tools. These new problems require the development of new conceptual constructs that will extend the capabilities of the discipline across a broad front and along many dimensions of new expertise. It will require an even higher order of information technology than is now on the drawing board.

Conceptual constructs for the application of management decision models have not, as a rule, been in the forefront of management scholars' considerations. They rarely appear in the current literature in explicit fashion—if they are present at all. Yet such constructs are implicit in the presentations of both theory and application.

There is a need to delineate the more applicable management principles, theories, practices, and logic found through a select survey of broad managerial literature areas, a management epistemology. This is necessary in order to identify critical and applicable management principles and practices to link the decision technology processes.

Decision formulating and modeling for management has yet to have its own well-defined epistemology. It is still fragmented; its techniques are piecemeal. Many of the techniques that exist are found outside the study of business; for example, economic, psychology, sociology, mathematics, computer sciences, control and feedback engineering, and production control.

IMPACTS OF FUTURE INFORMATION TECHNOLOGY DEVELOPMENTS ON DECISIONMAKING

It is important to look toward future advances in the technologies of computers and communications linked to knowledge processing and decision support systems. The computer complex for the 1990s will overcome many of the problems in today's decision systems. Some of these problems are

1. Computers were designed primarily for numerical computation and not for business decision processing.

2. The cost of hardware required a performance ratio that put emphasis on speed of central processing and larger memories.
3. The volume of software has increased to where it is almost impossible to organize and maintain efficiently.
4. Communications has not been effectively integrated with computers.

Today's managerial decision processes are limited. To deal with more complex problems, future managerial decision processes will require more knowledge about what is available and feasible. They will also require conversation in natural language as opposed to programming language, in which current software is written. Needed too is the ability to retrieve and use decision models with associative knowledge, data, and information bases including error analysis as well as the ability to retrieve and use pictorial and image data. A final requirement is the ability to compress data for decisionmaking in order to generate better alternative choices.

As we move toward the 1980s, we will need to become a knowledge-information processing society rather than a data-information processing society. In our highly developed technological culture, there are no longer any simple problems or issues. Even the design, manufacture, marketing, and sale of a toy produce a series of management decisions requiring the most sophisticated knowledge data bases and analysis techniques in order to assess the risk and rewards associated with this task.

The new academic discipline of creative and innovative management will evolve during the 1980s and 1990s and will play the central and most important role in the decisionmaking process. It will include organization and use of basic software systems, knowledge data base managerial systems, basic knowledge data bases, an intelligent interface system, and a problem-solving interface system, all working in harmony with the hardware system and in support of the decision function and our economic growth. What will it do for us? Among many things, it will

- Allow us to ask questions and get answers

- Organize our knowledge for the decision we want to make

- Provide office automation, computer-aided design, engineering, and instruction

- Use applied speech understanding
- Use applied problem solving

The impact of educating creative and innovative managers coupled with the effective use of future technology could be the step ahead for the nation to maintain the economic growth required to meet forecasted demands of society. In addition, creative and innovative management must be concerned with

- Distributed national and global networks with access to knowledge bases worldwide and intelligent, friendly interfaces with increased function and scope
- Measures of efficiency and flexibility for our institutions
- Decision support sciences and laboratories
- New expertise, relationships, and training
- Measures of the efficiency and effectiveness of management beyond return on investment, liquidity, work unit efficiency, and earnings per share
- Measures of effectiveness of current operations in meeting goals, technology transfer, development, and delivery of new products, goods, and services.

These impacts affect many of our current concerns and issues, but their realization depends on how we link our human and technological resources through creative and innovative managers.

AREAS FOR CREATIVE AND INNOVATIVE MANAGEMENT RESEARCH AND EXPERIMENTATION

It is difficult to launch a new discipline if one cannot delineate areas for research and experimentation. A core of the research can be started by working on selected current national problems. These problems are almost always broad and complex, require solutions within a reasonable period of time, demand cross-disciplinary talent and allocation of considerable resources. Their solutions often involve cooperation between government, business, labor, and educational institutions. The areas for effort include national security, the economy, environmental protection, education, use and reserving of natural resources, international trade, technology transfer, and a host of other matters.

What is called here *decision technology* is in Herb Simon's terminology "innovative research in non-programmed decisions." To quote him:

> Decision processes with these characteristics would be "unreasonable" under the conditions usually assumed in formal theories for rational choice. They become "reasonable" when we consider situations where the alternatives of choice are not given in advance, but must be discovered; where the means-ends connections between choices and consequences are imperfectly known, and must be explored; and finally, where a simplified and approximating frame of reference must be chosen before the choice can be brought within the limits of human computation.[5]

The problems that will form the basis of creative and innovative management as a new academic frontier can be characterized by one or more of the following:

1. Giant and dynamic-growth companies' corporate governance and their processes are radically changing from traditional decision-making and formal behavioral and organization theory to problems, issues, and initiative generation; e.g., nonprogrammed and technology decisionmaking with creativity and innovation.
2. An abundance, if not an overload, of creative technical and social inventions are available.
3. Occasions for innovations will occur under adverse conditions at the firm or national level because of international and domestic competition. The competition will be more than economic; it will include scientific advances, national security—defense and economic; and implementation of new technology into end products and services.
4. Choice criteria will be more than optimization or satisficing; it will include the use of power.

Specific matters for research are

- Wants versus needs—an economic analysis
- Public versus private communication systems
- Centralization versus decentralization—corporate governance
- Organization and distribution of information and technology

- Individual privacy versus the public's right to know
- "Real" versus "informational" environments—fact versus perceptions
- Managerial technology—application versus theory
- Newer organizational forms—governance and management styles

Academic Experimentation

Now is the time to experiment in developing the new frontier of creative and innovative management. There are two states to these experiments: (1) establish the goals; and (2) initiate interdisciplinary program in consonance with the goals.

One set of goals could be as follows:

1. To become a pacesetter for education for creative and innovative management in the context of a renewed American society
2. To train managers in the total environment of managing people, technology, and natural or replenishable resources on a state, national, and global basis
3. To develop innovative leadership on the part of faculties and administrations so as to delineate linkages between business on the one hand and the modern American capitalistic society on the other
4. To train managers to deal with global political and social changes
5. To see that managers learn to converse in appropriate foreign languages as well as the language of mathematics, statistics, and computer linguistics
6. To train managers to manage and use remote data bases
7. To understand and communicate with diverse and shifting constituencies
8. To set forth a modern and appropriate contextual economic role of private enterprise that removes the cultural contradictions of capitalism
9. To provide a renewed foundation of individual and institutional social values that are not based on hypocrisy and divergent standards for an institution and the individual
10. To establish basic areas for creative and innovative management that coordinates faculty research, the university research, the

academic curricula, teaching laboratories, and the recruitment of a high-quality, diversified, and representative student body dedicated to leadership responsibilities

11. To develop and make available unique and useful knowledge data bases that do not now exist

12. To develop analytical techniques, models, and simulations data that will provide a competitive capability for doing business in the arena of world markets

How do we measure success in meeting these goals? The clearest indication of an institution's value to society and the general welfare is to see who asks for its expertise, who wants the services of its students and faculty, and how often its contributions are locally, nationally, and internationally recognized.

Two critical issues need to be solved by the future leadership of business, government, educational institutions, and society as a whole. First, managing the future in terms of declines in sales and employment in our basic industries such as steel and automobiles, loss of overseas and domestic markets for low- and high-technology goods and services and changes in natural resource mix. Second, development of shared and desired goals for the management of resources, for the growth of wealth, and for income distribution.

An awareness of the interactions of science, technology, social, economic, political, and cultural factors on the constituencies of a society is evolving. The past two decades have seen a rapid transformation of American society in a way that challenges us to unify and disseminate ideals, values, and dreams and to use power in a constructive sense in the solution of societal problems.

The past can help us establish an understanding of a better future if we extract its lessons. Our combined intellectual capacities and individual experiences and capabilities will allow us to build a better society. These are times for bold pioneering—pioneering based on optimism but grounded in reality and with the determination to improve what exists and what will exist. We must do better in this period of rapid transition. It will be marked by national and international economic interdependencies. We can create this new discipline and the tools that are required to implement it. This is the time to dream of what can be.

NOTES TO CHAPTER 9

1. George Kozmetsky, "Society's Responsibility to Business as an Institution," presentation to the Southwest Division Board of Advisers Conference, U.S. Chamber of Commerce, Dallas, May 1975.
2. University of California, *Excellence in Education: An Opportunity and a Challenge*, 1963, p. 7.
3. Walt W. Rostow, *How It All Began: Origins for the Modern Economy*, (New York: McGraw-Hill, 1975), pp. 154–56.
4. Herbert A. Simon, *Models of Bounded Rationality: Behavioral Economics and Business Organizations*, vol. 2 (Cambridge, Mass.: MIT Press, 1982), p. 393.

10 CREATIVE AND INNOVATIVE MANAGEMENT
Its Future

We need a new breed of innovative managers. The need arises from both internal and external institutional factors. Internally, the major forces for change are the shrinking of middle management and the microgeneration of technologies that are altering the factory, the office, the professional workplace, and even the boardroom. Externally, these forces are our educational system and the burgeoning industrial infrastructure for governmental policies and regulations. Managers of all our institutions are facing pressures resulting from changes in American ideology, demographics, and public attitudes, concerns, and life-styles as well as demands imposed by the utilization of economic wealth and national resources, political philosophies, international trade barriers, and the rapid escalation of new clusters of technologies for the 1980s and 1990s. The consequences from this myriad of interlinking forces are real and extended to more than economic growth or stagnation. Indeed, the consequences may well determine the future form of our capitalistic society, the shifting socioeconomic make-up on our regions, the changing loci of American leadership and emerging interinstitutional networks.

Most managers have had difficulties relying on their experiences or drawing upon a theoretical framework for the economic recovery of their firms. This recovery will eventually lead to times when there can be acceptable employment or unemployment rates, higher profits, accessible capital markets at fair rates, controllable inflation, a

169

strong national security status, balanced international opportunities, an improved overall national research and development posture, and a reasonable quality of life. But innovative management must take the lead for this to happen.

DEFINITIONS

It is useful to differentiate between practical and academic knowledge. "Academic," from the Greek *Akademeia*, the gymnasium where Plato taught, means related or associated with an academy or school of higher learning; very learned but inexperienced in the world of practical reality; and theoretical without having an immediate bearing of practical or useful significance. *Practical*, from the Greek *prakitus*, 'to pass over,' 'to fare,' or 'to do,' means actively engaged in some course of action or occupation; being such in practice or effect; and disposed to action as opposed to speculation or obstruction.

There is no dichotomy between academic and practical management when both are used to fill the gap in management epistemology. *Epistomology*, from the Greek *epistene* 'knowledge or understanding' and *logos* 'study of,' is study of or a theory of the nature and grounds of knowledge with reference to its limits and validity.

TRANSFORMATION VERSUS TRANSITION

The first need in the 1980s for creative and innovative management is to understand that we are in a period of transformation and not simply transition. Today's managerial and economic uncertainties will not disappear by simply expanding our high-technology industries or revitalizing our basic industries. These are transitional processes. Gerhard Mensch has characterized the transition process as stalemate in technology. He aptly states that solutions to such stalemates occur only through social and technological innovations. This is what I refer to as a "transformation process."

Transformational managers are not merely power wielders eager to accomplish personal objectives but individuals who sense, direct, and provide the needs of followers. They are constantly aware that generation after generation fights to preserve the status quo. But status quo masks the fact that future well-being depends on the leadership capacity to recognize the need and the desirability to transform rather than cling to the familiar. In this context transformational managers in both emerging and mature firms must recognize that financial resources must be converted to produce wealth in a timely fashion and used to create newer institutional linkages that not only meet the prioritized needs of the firm but also contribute to the well-being of our region and our nation.

The transformation process must take into account the fact that emerging technologies will be our nation's newer growth industries stimulating a robust economy during the next decade. What must still be reviewed is whether creative and innovative management will be capable of providing significantly greater employment of the working force, over the whole gamut of skills and education, while at the same time maintaining a balanced economic structure for national defense and prestige.

Another source of transformation includes the technologies for the Fourth Industrial Revolution: microelectronics, biotechnology, lasers, artificial intelligence and robotics, synthetic materials, waste technologies and communications (see Table 10–1). These and other innovations in the next few decades will lead to markets for advanced materials, special application designs, photosynthesis, supercold technology, industrial and scientific instrumentation, robots, and automated batch and process production. All of these Fourth Industrial Revolution technologies should lead to long-term investments in newer plants and equipment, increased productivity and a stronger U.S. international trade posture.

Commercialization is the process by which the results of research and development are transformed into the marketplace as products and services. It is the essential means for changing a society through managing transformational sources and needs. Commercialization requires the interchange of ideas and opinions that are technological in nature—choices between technology-making and technology-taking. Today's conference will place more emphasis for management needs in the 1980s on technology-taking. The taking is in terms of entrepreneurship, interfirm cooperation, venture capital formation, establishment of university-based development centers, valuing the new technology, and monitoring technology trends. Commercialization also helps to define the educational and training requirements for present and emerging marketplaces. It can thus be a major driving

Table 10-1. Technology Now and Tomorrow.

1. Microelectronics	(a) Advanced chips, very high speed integrated circuits (VHSIC)
	(b) Advanced software applications
	(c) Personal computers
	(d) Distributed computing
	(e) Unique Databases
2. Medicine	(a) Biotechnology
	(b) Psychotherapy
	(c) Transplantation
	(d) Birth control
	(e) Genetic Engineering
	(f) Medical electronics
3. Materials	(a) Special application designs
	(b) Photosynthesis
	(c) Supercold technology
4. Industrial and Scientific Instruments	(a) Robotics
	(b) Automated batch production
	(c) Control electronics
5. Energy	(a) Solar
	(b) Fusion
	(c) Coal technology
	(d) Satellite power stations
	(e) Geothermal
	(f) Biomass
6. Defense technologies	(a) Electronic warfare
	(b) Nuclear
	(c) Biological
	(d) Economic
7. Agricultural technologies	(a) Genetic modification and selection
	(b) Electrostatic spraying
	(c) Waste management
	(d) Nuclear radiation
8. Water	(a) Desalinization
	(b) Growth regulation
	(c) Conservation
	(d) Weather modification
	(e) Transportation
9. Other	(a) Airwaves and communication
	(b) Construction
	(c) Transportation

force that invigorates newer industries and rejuvenates senior industries. Commercialization is also a measure of the extent and effectiveness of creative and innovative management in each stage of the
process.

Technology, like *innovation*, is a much overused word. It is, therefore, appropriate to ask, "How does technology originate?" As Professor Mensch has written, it does not simply "fall from heaven." His
basic assumption is that "Man is a tool-making animal." He has also
stated that "the individual and organized human capabilities for
technology-making and technology-taking will determine the course
of events in the coevolution of technology and society." What is clear
is that institutions are performing basic research, applied research,
and developmental research that result in scientific knowledge and
technical know-how as well as products and services that are ready
to be marketed. They are commercialized through product development, intrapreneurship, entrepreneurship, capital venturing, university development centers, and robust growth companies.

Transforming science into a technological resource has been predominantly entrusted to scientists and advanced engineers. It is not
yet generally recognized as a managerial responsibility.

There are a set of institutions that are sources for R&D—government, industry, and nonprofit institutions. There are others that are
the performers of R&D—government laboratories, industry, universities and colleges, and other nonprofit institutions.

Although scientific knowledge is reposited in schools, libraries,
and a variety of other public and private institutions, the transformation of science to a technological resource is not yet a well-defined
academic field. The transfer of technical knowledge to technological
resources is a better understood process. Technical knowledge is
transformed into patents and then subsequent licensing and cross-
licensing agreements and multinational corporations have produced a
wholesale transfer of scientific and technological knowledge across
national frontiers. The efficiency and effectiveness as well as the flexibility and adaptability of the transformation of scientific and technological knowledge into practically useful resources are to the best
of my knowledge a fresh area for academic research. Because of the
importance of this emerging area to the nation, it currently has come
under increasing scrutiny from national security and international
trade perspectives.

Basic research—scientific knowledge and breakthroughs—is perhaps
less subject to security restrictions and is still predominantly thought

of in Jeffersonian terms as a "free world good." Even with relatively free access of all institutions and nations to scientific breakthroughs, the actual implementation, or commercialization of the emerging technologies is dependent upon the degree of stagnation in the old technologies and the attractiveness of the new alternatives.

Creative and innovative management must face several critical issues in the future.

1. *Technology transfer will most often not be things but know-how, the demonstration of feasibility, the process of planning, and the mechanism of manufacturing.* The concept is more attitudinal than tangible, more principle than product. Manufacturing technology, for example, should be encouraged in a cooperative effort between industry and government. Legal aspects must be clarified and simplified—the patent process, the classification process, and the Freedom of Information Act in juxtaposition to proprietary company data.

2. *The commercialization process demands particular expertise not necessarily transferable directly within the same organization.* It is not required that a defense-oriented firm develop its own technology and bring it to market. Corporate cultures are different; a market sense is often an art unfamiliar to military contractors and it may be socially inefficient for some to develop it. Alternative approaches should make frequent use of the licensing of technology and the subcontracting of marketing and manufacturing.

3. *Mechanisms must be developed to maximize individual entrepreneurial motivation while optimizing collective social benefits.* Incentive generation is vital. Research and innovation are not the same thing; the former can be done on demand, the latter cannot. Research can be programmed from without, innovation must be motivated from within. Public policy must accord inventors and innovators in all sectors—industry, university, government—full rights to their creations; anything less will restrict the process and retard the economy. There is need for entrepreneurial education, the teaching of students, the instruction of practitioners. There is also need for long-term thinking among large-company chief executive officers; CEOs must be encouraged to see even beyond their own tenures of office.

4. *We must establish a compelling cooperative relationship among business, universities, and government.* Incentives must inherently

motivate each sector to interact without external coercion. The old order was shattered in the 1960s; a new one must be structured in the 1980s. It is not sufficient for professors to go off into industry to do their most productive work. Our future research base demands the guided supervision of first-rate graduate students and this means strong on-campus incentives for first-rate faculty. There is critical need for undirected, nonclassified, pure scientific research—which can occur only in universities and should never be controlled. To establish and maintain American leadership in science and technology, we must create environments for intellectual entrepreneurship, and the financial energy to drive the system must come from government. Properly facilitating mechanism—overcoming the inertia of implementation—is a prime responsibility of the new partnership.

5. *The states must play an active role in the commercialization process; decentralization of control is essential.* Mechanisms must be found to encourage the active participation of state government in the transfer cycle; closer touch with local business will facilitate the development of effective programs.

6. *We must maintain awareness of the social consequences of changing technology.* A new breed of managers—schooled in the sciences and sensitive to the humanities—must be trained to assume leadership roles. They must become appreciative of the participants—customers, workers, citizens. It is conventional wisdom that business should become more of a science; true, but business will forever remain an art, an art that should employ more science. The man-machine interface must tilt to the man; we must become acclimated to change; transparent technology must foster, not inhibit, human creativity. Imaginative and projective mechanisms should be developed to anticipate the future. Today's critical need is not more data, but less. We are struggling against an enormous tide of information. We require data-reduction techniques more than ones of accumulation. We need directed analysis, the intelligent search for meaning.

7. *Business schools sit at the interface among industry, university, and government and should influence intersector interaction.* The responsibilities of academic business faculties have broad social impact. Business is the economic synthesis of human knowledge. The advancement of business knowledge is quite literally the growth of society. In this regard, business faculties occupy a unique position in the academic constellation. They have special opportunity to integrate and synthesize research from diverse areas. Work coming out of

the physical, biological, and social sciences is all germane to business investigation and becomes the substrate from which new concepts and creations are fashioned. Similarly, the potential interaction among academic, corporate, and government R&D offers critical mass potential for generating new ideas, ventures, and systems. If economic development is dependent on the birth of new knowledge, then the gestation should take place in business schools.

To deal with these issues, transformational managers should consider several initiatives that can accelerate the commercialization process.

1. *Enact a National Commercialization Act (NCA).*   NCA would authorize the formation of public/private joint technology ventures, create a national technology strategy mechanism, target technology to domestic and international markets, stimulate new technology-based industries and invest seed monies when required because of public need or because of the nature of the risk-taking. Legislation would make the implementation feasible by specifically permitting public/private joint ventures in which the federal and state governments would be limited equity partners. In all circumstances, however, the individual enterprises would be managed and primarily owned by the private sector.

2. *Public and private sector managers should adopt a policy to broaden their allocation of R&D funds both geographically and institutionally.*   Broadening the base of producers of R&D will extend the range of commercialization of technology. More important, it can surmount the current deficit of doctoral level scientists and engineers in a minimum of time. It will, in addition, help to utilize more productively current academic resources that are already in place. Broadening the base of producers can help to overcome what can be regarded as critical regional economic inequities.

3. *Managers should encourage the adoption of policies and regulations to provide maximum access to government funded basic research.*   The United States must reestablish its lead in world technology. The Department of Defense is a major organization with the reason, the leadership, and the resources to help accomplish this. DOD must be the critical driving force in supporting university and industrial R&D. Full cooperation between DOD, universities, and industry is absolutely essential.

4. *Managers should advocate the modification of antitrust laws or the development of new regulations to encourage joint efforts for research and development.* Several key factors can facilitate joint efforts: a) companies involved in joint research efforts must commit funding of R&D for an extended period of time (three to five years); b) these funds must be earmarked for at least one aspect of the joint research; c) patents should be held in the name of the joint research corporation with participants having a set lead time for commercialization; d) special provisions should be made for small and medium company participation; and e) an accountability program should be instituted that requires self-certification.

5. *Managers should take advantage of tax and other selected investment policies for innovation to encourage investments for dynamic and productive growth industries.* There are three key investment policies available to managers: a) write off obsolete capital equipment faster than current schedules permit; b) utilize financial free trade zones; and c) bolster international trade by taking advantage of the Export–Import Bank.

6. *Managers should advocate the elimination of taxation from long-term capital gains as a means of increasing investments.*

7. *Managers should encourage pension and other funding groups to invest in innovative technologies being transferred to commercial ventures.*

The ability to take scientific knowledge and technical know-how and convert them into technology resources is an extremely creative managerial process. But this process is little understood. Any breakthrough can well provide practical management "know-how" for national and international leadership, increased wealth and the identification of productive investments that will positively transform our society.

INDEX

ABOUT THE AUTHOR

Dr. George Kozmetsky served as Dean of the University of Texas College of Business Administration and Graduate School of Business from 1966 to 1982. He continues to be Director of UT's IC² Institute and holder of the endowed J. Marion West Chair in Constructive Capitalism. He also has the rank of professor in the Departments of Management and Computer Sciences.

Dr. Kozmetsky is former corporate Vice-President of Litton Industries, and was cofounder and Executive Vice-President of Teledyne, Inc. He has served as Chairman of the Board and President of the Institute of Management Sciences, and as director of numerous institutions and corporations, including the Adlai Stevenson Institute for International Affairs. Among his books are *Funds Management and Managerial Research*, coauthored with Isabella Cunningham; *Information Technology: Initiatives for Today—Decisions That Cannot Wait*, coauthored with Timothy W. Ruefli; and *Making it Together: A Survival Manual for the Executive Family*, coauthored with Ronya Kozmetsky.